*The illustration depicts Abraham Lincoln and his youngest
son Tad, photographed in 1864 not reading the Bible
(see pp. 136–7)*

For
Julian Bach of New York City
and
Hilary Rubinstein of London

Author's Note

Sometimes this book takes liberties with the order of events, but there is a chronology at the back to set things straight.

It is shamelessly indebted, as anyone can tell, to the researches of more scholarly writers. To all of them, living or dead, I offer my respectful and apologetic gratitude.

Trefan Morys, 1999

Contents

Preconceptions: Grape Jelly

I thought of calling this book *Grape Jelly*.

'*Grape Jelly!* What kind of a title would that have been, for a book about Mr Lincoln?'

I will tell you how it was. Two things I turned against, when I first arrived in the United States of America during the Presidency of Dwight D. Eisenhower. One was grape jelly. I was spending a year wandering at will around the country, staying mostly at cheap motels and eating my breakfasts at nearby diners or coffee shops. Addict as I was of bitter orange marmalade with my toast, I was dismayed to discover that nearly everywhere all that was available was something called grape jelly, sealed in Cellophane. I had never tasted it before. I know now that some grape jellies are delicious, but the ones I had then were horrible. They seemed to represent all that I distrusted about America: synthetic, over-sweet, slobbery of texture, artificially coloured and unavoidable.

The other thing that antagonized me was the myth of

Abraham Lincoln. It seemed to me in the early 1950s that the American people as a whole were almost deranged in their obsession with their sixteenth President, the country boy from the Middle West who, by overcoming the rebel South in the American civil war, had ended American slavery and saved the Union. He had been assassinated at the moment of victory almost a century before, but he seemed to me, as a brash young European, all too intrusively alive. I could not evade him and his saintly image. He cropped up in all the conversations by which kind Americans tried to introduce me to the meaning of their country, and he seemed to stare down at me monumentally in every other public place, with a mixture of the judgemental, the homespun and the sanctimonious that I came to find intolerable.

These inescapable images everywhere, the reverent and often obsequious way people talked about him, the Lincoln books that were piled in every bookstore, the sickly log-cabin-to-White House legend that entwined him, the very way Americans referred to him as 'Mr Lincoln', when he was dead and gone before most of their grandparents were born, and was surely only another party politician anyway – all this, together with my own youthful prejudices against ostentatiously self-made men, cottage philosophers, role models, mimics, comic racon-teurs and the University of Life, amazed and depressed me, and made me view Mr Lincoln with a decidedly sceptic eye.

I realize now that I was witnessing the zenith of Lincoln's myth, the years after the Second World War when he was regarded as a very metaphor of the benign and victorious Republic. Stoked with the propaganda of war and victory, unprecedentedly prosperous, flushed with success, gleaming and glittering above the world's debris, the United States saw itself as a supreme example for all humanity. It had demonstrated once and for all that a democratic State could not only govern itself better than any other, but could also overcome the worst of perils without sacrificing its liberties or its values. It was how the whole planet ought to be, and it saw its ideology as Lincoln's own. His famous phrases exactly suited the moment and its rhetoric – 'The last best hope of earth', 'Right makes might', 'With malice towards none', 'Of the people, by the people, for the people'.

Politicians of both the great parties claimed Lincoln as their inspiration then. At a time when racial segregation was still absolute in some American States, the most militant black leaders revered his memory. Thirty new books about Lincoln had appeared in 1950 alone, but the work the Ladies' Literary Circles seemed to be discussing, wherever I went, was Carl Sandburg's six-volume biography, which had been published between 1926 and 1939 and had become a testament of the nation's high-flown self-image, much of it being couched in an ineffably mannered poetical prose. The idea of war itself was given a Lincolnian stamp – had not Mr Lincoln sanctified the most dreadful of civic conflicts as a kind of crusade for the freedom of the slaves, just as the Second World War had been fought for the liberation of all mankind? Aaron Copland had written his tone-poem *Lincoln Portrait* specifically as a contribution to the war effort.

The nearest to Lincoln lese-majesty I remember in the 1950s was Oliver Jensen's affectionate parody of the Gettysburg Address in the style of President Eisenhower – 'I haven't checked the figures but eighty-seven years ago, I think it was, a number of individuals organized a government set-up here in this country . . .' Otherwise all was hushed respect. Survivors of the civil war were still available for inspirational interviews, and now and then there entered the newspapers somebody who had actually set eyes on Abraham Lincoln – had even met him, like the centenarian Henry Hendon of New York, who had shaken the Lincoln hand ninety years before. 'Why do we love this man,' asked an advertisement for the John Hancock Mutual Life Insurance Company, 'dead long before our time, yet dear to us as a father?' Because, the advertisement answered itself, 'he was everybody, grown a little taller – the warm and living proof of our American faith that greatness comes out of everywhere when it is free to come.'

It seemed to me a sort of sententious mania, akin to the obsession of the old Venetians with their patron chimera, the Lion of St Mark. It was actually the climax of a deliberate process that had begun with Lincoln's murder on Good Friday, 1865. Transfiguration had started at once, as though the American people had instinctively decided that they needed a new Redeemer. The triumphs of the 1775 revolution had been overshadowed by the civil war, and its heroes had lost some of their semi-divine allure. Lincoln was their obvious successor, as the Saviour of the Union, the Great Emancipator, the original All-

American. When he died the legend arose that the clocks in watchmakers' windows, habitually set at 7.22 the best to display their faces, had miraculously stopped then to mark the moment of his martyrdom. A funeral train of seven black coaches carried his shrouded catafalque in solemn progress across the nation, pausing at cities and towns along the way for mourning ceremonies and orations. And when they buried him at last in his home town, Springfield, Illinois, then what a flood of tragic celebration was released! Colonel Robert Hamer of Vermont, Illinois, in whose house Lincoln had once spent a night, instantly had the entire building repainted black, and all across the Republic municipalities vied with each other to express their devotion (except in the defeated and still bitter South, where one man shot himself in disgust at all this 'servile sycophancy').

The plaques, the memorials, the renaming of streets! The odes that were spouted down the years, the novels and plays that were written, the music that was composed, the engravings that were engraved, the outpouring of memoirs, the dedication of commemorative fountains, parks, libraries, gardens and public halls! Lincoln's birthplace became a national shrine, his most famous speeches were incised in bronze. Thirty-five American towns and cities, twenty-two counties, were named after him. The first transcontinental road was the Lincoln Highway. At least 125 statues were erected in his honour: in Illinois he was a clean-cut young pioneer, in Newark, New Jersey, he sat pensive on a park bench, in North Dakota he was colossal on Mount Rushmore and in Washington he became the dominant figure of a lapidary city, on a high marble throne above a reflecting pool, like a judge of judges or a god-king. At Disneyland in California his animated image was capable of performing 275,000 possible combinations of facial expressions and body movements. He was to figure in 130 movies – Walter Huston, Henry Fonda and Raymond Massey were all cinematic Lincolns in their time (though most Americans would probably have seen him more as a cross between James Stewart and John Wayne).

Some 10,000 Lincoln titles were presently catalogued in the Library of Congress, and there were two Lincoln encyclopedias. His was the first Presidential profile to appear on the United States coinage – the most frequently reproduced portrait in the world – and his image would grace stamps and banknotes for ever after. The cartoon persona of Old Abe became almost indistinguishable from Uncle Sam himself; even his assassination launched a perennial American genre, the conspiracy theory. An expensive automobile ('The Car of Presidents'), a kind of rocking-chair, a variety of rose, a tomato, a tunnel under the Hudson River, a battalion of volunteers in the Spanish Civil War, an opera house, a submarine, an aircraft carrier – all were named in his honour. Relays of academics assessed and reassessed his story, analysing and debating every detail of his life and character, exploring Oedipal rivalries with the Founding Fathers, attending Lincoln seminars, contributing to Lincoln symposia and sometimes conveniently intermarrying. Generations of American schoolchildren devoted projects to Father Abraham, and at the end of the twentieth century were still besieging websites with inquiries such as (I quote verbatim): 'Do you think he would of died if we had the meddical technology today? If so how long do you think he would of lived for then.'

A literary industry arose around the Lincoln memory, until it could be said that more words had been written about him than about anyone else except Jesus Christ, to whom he was frequently likened – for example, on an obelisk at Council Bluffs, Iowa, where he was described as

> *A King of Men*
> *Whose Crown was Love*
> *Whose Throne was Gentleness.*

If the United States were an older country fragments of his bones, shrivelled fingernails and locks of hair would have been preserved in reliquaries and credited with miraculous cures.

Is it any wonder that when I arrived in the United States at the apex of this idolatry, I found it all rather overwhelming? It went against my grain, as a European and a natural iconoclast. Surely there was something phoney to it all, something trumped-up and ersatz – rather like that damned grape jelly, in fact. For nearly half a century I intermittently thought about Abraham Lincoln and his reputation, wondering if I had been fair in these original responses, if he really had been the saint he was made out to be, or was just another political opportunist riding the tides of democracy. I went to America often, but could never quite make up my mind about him: and so in the end I resolved to get to know the sixteenth President a little more intimately, to follow his life and career wherever it took him, and eventually to make a book of it.

Having reached this decision, one day during a café breakfast in California I told a woman at the next table of my old bigotry against grape jelly (frequently offered by then in a plastic package called a Flav-r-Savr), and how I had come to equate it with the myth of Abraham Lincoln. She was horrified – more than horrified, actually *distressed*. She almost burst into tears. Grape jelly! Why, she said, when she was a little girl, living in Brooklyn with her immigrant parents from Eastern Europe, grape jelly was the one single touch of luxury her family could afford. It was the promise of America, her mother's comfort, her father's pride. It was the sweet American Dream, symbolizing all that was hopeful about the Great Republic. How could I speak like that of grape jelly? Had I no heart?

I was touched and confounded by this exchange, and did not pursue the Lincoln parallel. I knew that in so passionately defending the jelly, she was defending the icon too – for her as for me, although in a very different way, the two were analogous. But when the time came I dropped that title anyway.

One

Hingham in Norfolk, England, is where Abraham Lincoln's paternal forebears came to America from, his father's great-great-grandfather having emigrated to the colonies in the late seventeenth century. It is a trim country village with a fine fourteenth-century church, some handsome eighteenth-century houses, a couple of inns, a Methodist chapel and a main road running through it. Unlike most English villages nowadays, it supports a thriving community of craftsmen and shopkeepers, and it used to bask in the local nickname 'Little London'.

Generations of Lincolns, we are told, lived in the ancillary hamlet of Swanton Morley, first in a cottage, then in a grander house which is now absorbed into the Angel Inn; a grassy plot of land behind the pub is preserved by the National Trust in not very evocative remembrance – it looks like a small bowling green. In Hingham church, amidst sundry Lincoln references and suitably embroidered hassocks, there is a bust of Abraham on a wall, presented by the citizens of Hingham, Massachusetts, and excellent cream teas are served at Lincoln's Tea and Coffee Shoppe along the road. All in all Hingham is a tasteful, steady, very Saxon sort of place, and the best-known British writer about Abraham Lincoln, Lord Charnwood, liked to think he could trace his hero's character to his Norfolk origins. He was of sound English rural stock, Charnwood thought, and it is true that to this day Lincoln's gaunt and lanky frame, his pinched face and his Anglo-Saxon attitudes sometimes do show among country people of East Anglia.

On the other hand, away to the west in the wild moorlands of north Wales stands a derelict farmhouse called Bryn Gwyn, near the hill-hamlet of Ysbyty Ifan, which is a place of quite another kind. It is a magical place. Fairies and magicians abounded there long ago, and princes, and elegiac bards! Melancholy songs were sung to the harp! Slippery tricks were played, ambiguous tales were told at firesides! A terrific prospect extends to the west from Bryn Gwyn, away to the clumped mountains of Eryri, white with snow in winter, blue-grey on a summer day. Not another house is to be seen from the old building, and nobody has lived here since the 1940s, but fine big ash trees stand guard behind it, and nearby are the barn and sheep-pen where today's farmer shears his sheep and piles his black plastic packages of silage.

There are no mementoes of Abraham Lincoln here, no fancy hassocks or scones for tea, but from Bryn Gwyn in the 1660s, so brave Welsh genealogists assure us, Elen Morys and her husband Cadwaladr Evans emigrated to America, where they became the sixteenth President's maternal great-great-great-grandparents. Charnwood liked to think of Lincoln as a Norfolk yeoman, but I am a Welsh Morys myself, with an Evans grandmother, and I prefer to see in him the charisma of a high Welsh heritage; for those Welsh scholars swear too that Cadwaladr Evans was collaterally related to Rhodri Fawr the King of Gwynedd and even to Owain Glyndŵr, greatest of all Welsh patriots, who vanished from human ken in the fifteenth century never to be seen again. Let Lord Charnwood keep that patch of mown grass behind the Angel Inn, courtesy of the National Trust. Give me, for my Lincoln memorial, the windswept ruin of Bryn Gwyn, where princes ride and poets sadly sing.

Not that it matters anyway. Most Americans have long since forgotten that Lincoln's forebears came from anywhere but the USA; Lincoln himself was not greatly interested in his European ancestry, and might indeed have been amused by the tradition that he was descended from a nameless foundling deposited on the doorstep of Lincoln's Inn, the ancient London legal society. He was a child of the untamed American backwoods, and his more immediate origins are generally described as ambivalent, partly because his line has been complicated by births out of recorded wedlock, partly because people have found it hard to believe that so towering a statesman could emerge from so obscure a background, and partly because Lincoln himself was reluctant to talk about it all.

Academic controversy has raged over the manner of his upbringing in the American West of the early nineteenth century – the Middle West of today. Nobody seems to know for sure what kind of people the Lincolns were. Were they predominantly (1) poor but respectable, (2) come down in the world, (3) comfortably land-owning by the standards of the time and place, (4) hardily pioneering or (5) rock-bottom bucolic? Investigators have argued all five cases, producing (Case 1) records of regular Lincoln chapel attendance, (Case 2) genteel Lincoln relatives back east, (Case 3) sizeable Lincoln property holdings, (Case 4) folk-memories of true-blue Lincoln conduct or (Case 5) evidence of unlovely Lincoln circumstances. Abraham Lincoln himself adhered to Case 5, with occasional deviations in the direction of Virginia gentry. Asked once to talk about his early life, he said there was nothing much to talk about – it was just 'the simple annals of the poor'. Asked another time, he said his boyhood was 'stinted', by which he meant it was arid, philistine and deprived.

He is also apocryphally quoted as saying that his family was 'white trash'. This was a phrase devised by the black people of the American South, in the days before political correctness, to describe their indigent white neighbours, whom they considered endemically lazy and unreliable. It is still a convenient if prejudiced generic for many inhabitants of Lincoln's native region. His father Thomas (part farmer, part carpenter) had migrated with his wife Nancy (née Hanks) in an apparently somewhat listless way out of Virginia into the northern part of Kentucky, and to this day those poor hill regions, on the edge of the Bible Belt, on the border between North and South, form a white trash homeland. It is exemplified, in my own mind, by hugely bulbous young mothers in trousers smoking cigarettes, by the peculiar stale smell of down-market motel rooms, by junk food of awful malnutrition, by trailers parked in messy woodlands, by dubious evangelical preachers and six-packs of tasteless beer and abandoned cars with grass growing over them and TV game shows and lugubrious Country and Western music thumping out of pick-up trucks.

Was this the kind of society, *mutatis mutandis*, into which Abraham Lincoln was born, in the days when the American frontier, with its volatile mixture of the bold, the Godly, the shady and the plain riff-raff, was fitfully pushing westward out of the Appalachian mountains? His friend and devoted biographer William Herndon defined it as 'a stagnant, putrid pool', and hardly more than thirty years after the Revolution, life was certainly rough and ready at these limits of civilization. The western frontier States were still covered with forests and more or less roadless, while beyond them the vast continent was an inchoate mass of sparsely settled terri-tories, mostly unexplored; New Orleans, bought from the French in 1803, was the solitary big city out there. Scattered Indians were the only people who had lived in the frontier regions for more than a generation: all the white people were migrants or settlers in flux – sometimes

aiming to stay in a place for good, sometimes only in
transit towards more promising country over the hill. If
they wanted meat they shot or slaughtered it. If they
wanted whiskey they distilled it. Protestant chapels
proliferated, served by zealous and sometimes fanatical
ministers, but here as in the Europe of the time innumerable superstitions governed the conduct of simple people
– the malice of moon-phases, the ominous influence of
birds, breath of horses, witches' spells, hex and shibboleth,
potion and philtre and magic cure. A fastidious Easterner
passing this way in 1818 described the people, men,
women and children, as 'wallowing in promiscuous filth'.

   He was certainly piously exaggerating (his name was
Elias P. Fordham). All the same, even in the 1950s, when
my family and I spent some time in the American South,
the poor whites next door to us lived appallingly sordid
lives, in rooms full of cockroaches and discarded beer
cans, beating their children at the drop of a one-eyed
teddy-bear and shouting abuse at each other late into the
night. In those days they were too thin rather than too
fat, scrawny and ill-nourished, and this now makes it all
the easier for me to imagine little Lincoln growing up
among their mess and screamed invectives. Patriotic
chroniclers would be horrified at the fancy. They present
the Lincoln clan as honest, diligent and God-fearing
pioneers, and there were undeniably respectable burghers
among Lincoln's relatives. But his mother is generally
agreed nowadays to have been illegitimate (and herself
no better than she ought to have been, so neighbours
said), while his father Thomas was characterized by a
contemporary as 'an excellent specimen of white trash'

—lazy, worthless, slow-moving and slow-talking. Lincoln *père* was a practising Baptist but an unsuccessful defendant in four lawsuits, and 'from what I hear,' an informant told me in Lexington, Kentucky, a century and a half later, 'when he got old he was meaner'n a rattlesnake.'

Anyway to my mind the Lincoln legend is far more striking if its hero sprang allegorically from the cloaca. Fortunately nothing could be much more allegorical than the famous one-room log cabin in which he was born, at Sinking Spring Farm near Hodgenville in Kentucky. We are told that his mother, in her labour, lay close to its smoky fire on a bed of corn husks and bearskins, above a floor of dried mud (his father being too shiftless to make floorboards): and that thus, on 12 February 1809, little Abe entered what Carl Sandburg was characteristically to call a world of 'whispering dreams and wistful dust'.

Whether it really is that log cabin is open to doubt. *Some* of its logs are *probably* genuine, is all its National Park Service guardians claim, and scoffers like to remember the joke that says Lincoln was born in a log cabin he had built with his own hands. But the hut has played the role for so long, has convinced so many millions of visitors, that like many another place of pilgrimage it has by now acquired the aura if not of fact, at least of faith. It certainly looks uncomfortable enough to ring true; although entirely scrubbed and empty now, it could easily be fitted out with mud, corn husks, bearskins and wistful dust, if not with whispering dreams. It was an original progenitor of those trailers in the woods: if

Lincoln were to be born today, he would be born in a mobile home.

Several cabins more or less like it, all purporting to have housed the young Lincoln or members of his family at one time or another, are scattered through northern Kentucky, up through Indiana and into Illinois, and are linked by roadside markers and tourist brochures into something called the Lincoln Heritage Trail. Imagine the labour of it, when the Lincolns moved to another farm, probably because of some squabble about land rights, as they loaded their implements on the wagons once again, and plodded off into the west! It is bad enough even now, as one sweeps across these landscapes in a comfortable car. The forests may have been tamed, the roads are splendid, but sometimes there is still nothing but woodland for hours on end, and sometimes only a dull flat countryside littered with trailers and with the neon signs, mounted on tall pillars like saints in a medieval desert, which announce the imminence of yet another McDonald's, Pizza Hut, Wendy's or Comfort Inn. There are few surprises along the Lincoln Trail through Kentucky and Indiana. There are no handsome old market towns. There are no sudden lakes or mountains. There are very few bookshops. Theatres and concert halls are almost unknown. The height of gastronomic aspiration I found, during a journey in 1998, was an Indiana cream torte defined as 'a yellow cake with rich milk chocolate *ganache*, sweet raspberry marmalade and smooth pastry cream, iced with Italian butter-cream'. Half the houses, pretending to be white colonial-style clapboard, are really made of plastic over breeze-blocks.

Horizons are still so limited that when I once told a shopkeeper I came from Britain, she said I must have lived in the United States for a long time, because I spoke such fluent English.

Sinking Spring to Knob Creek, Little Pigeon Creek to Macon County, as I potter myself from one to the other, imagining them as they must have been 150 years ago, they strike me as memorials of a dispiriting childhood.

In children's hagiographies the boy Lincoln is portrayed as an idealized Huck Finn, shoeless but merry, manfully fetching water from the well, gazing into his Mom's eyes as she tells stories from the Bible, cheerfully helping his Daddy to chop wood or pick pumpkins. Sometimes the family certainly settled in countryside that now looks lovely, all dogwood and green oaks, rushing trout streams and meadows humming with congenial insects; little Abe must have got his share of fun out of a wilderness childhood – fishing, collecting berries, wandering the woods, climbing trees and falling into streams. But in the early 1800s, when the whole country was scarcely inhabited, and families like the Lincolns had to hack and scratch a living out of a forested wasteland, for ever ploughing, hoeing, building fences or shooting turkeys, to an intelligent and imaginative boy a lifetime in these parts must have seemed an uninviting prospect. He felt, so he said in later years, 'an utter lack of any romantic or heroic elements', and Indiana, where the Lincolns settled longest, was 'as unpoetical as any spot of the earth'.

For of course he was not, as that insurance company advertisement claimed, just 'everybody, grown taller'. Every gossipy recollection that has come down to us from his childhood emphasizes how different he was from everyone else. Much of this folklore is unreliable, having been dredged out of the past years after the event, or even invented for profit or effect – an amazing number of ancients were discovered to have had contact with the young Lincoln, when he became the martyred President of their nation. Some recollections, though, are convincing. Abraham certainly looked odd from the start: so tall and ungainly, with such big feet and long arms, that some researchers have postulated a kind of endocrine abnormality. He liked to carry a stick, with a beechwood head he had carved himself. He was immensely strong, and a keen wrestler – an enthusiasm inherited, it is said, from his mother Nancy Hanks, who like some Welsh women of the time was apparently an able wrestler herself. He was insatiably inquisitive, sometimes infuriating his father by butting into adult affairs and conversations. It is true I am sure that he learnt to read precociously early, giving him an almost mystic prestige in that community of illiterates. By frontier standards he was lazy, always preferring a book to a hammer, and one cannot for a moment doubt his para-doxically tender love for animals, which lasted all his life. This surfaced in his eighth year when, having shot a wild turkey as every frontier urchin must, he found himself mourning its death: down the years horses, dogs, pigs, goats, racoons, terrapins, and especially cats and kittens were all befriended by Abe Lincoln, and it was perhaps no coincidence that when he got to the White House, a pet turkey was among the family ménage.

This was not how 'everybody' behaved, especially in that wild environment of the backwoods. Because the boy Lincoln was so clearly remarkable, and so frank about it, he got away with his differences. People liked him. He was tough and self-reliant, which obviously helped with his peers, and he told entertaining stories. Even his congenital physical idleness seems to have been forgiven a prodigy who could actually write the neighbours' letters for them. Still, he was always one of a kind – if not isolated, sometimes surely lonely. How could such a lively, wondering mind confine itself to the planting of vegetables or the slaughter of poor birds? Lincoln was to grow into a quixotic personality in many ways, and in his frequent moments of depression he was truly a knight of the mournful countenance – 'melancholy dripped from him as he walked', Herndon famously wrote long afterwards. Deposited in those unlyrical parts, in crammed log cabins hardly larger than prison cells, no wonder little Abe grew up sad.

Besides, calamity after calamity befell him in his back-woods childhood. His circle of acquaintances was deci-mated by the dreadful milk sickness (modern brucellosis, perhaps), caught from cows which had grazed the poison-ous snakeroot. His only brother died when he was three. His mother died when he was nine, and he is said to have helped make her coffin. When he was seventeen one of his friends went mad. When he was nineteen his sister died. Cousins and neighbours collapsed all around him. His father appears to have drifted from one half-cock

enterprise to another; bankrupts and ne'er-do-wells frequented his earliest years. Everyone was illiterate, or
nearly so, and Lincoln had a total of one year's elementary
schooling at most – among his kind of people, as he said
himself, 'there was absolutely nothing to excite ambition
for education.'

Most of his childhood he spent slaving away at menial
family tasks: 'an axe was put into his hand,' he wrote
about himself in retrospect, 'and with the trees and
logs and grubs he fought until his 20th year'. His chief
consolation seems to have been provided by his kind and
sensible stepmother, the widowed Sarah Bush Johnston,
whom Thomas brought into the Indiana woods, poor
soul, just a year after Nancy's death, together with two
daughters and a no-good son to be jammed into the log
cabin of the moment. The new Mrs Lincoln was unable
to write her own name, but she brought with her a
few books, and these provided the real basis of Abe's
education. They were an eclectic but invigorating mix,
including the King James Bible, *Robinson Crusoe*, some
simplified and doubtless bowdlerized version of *The
Thousand and One Nights*, Mason Locke Weems' epic
Life and Memorable Actions of George Washington ('There
the battling armies met in thunder – the stormy strife
was short'), and Webster's Speller, which also contained
improving maxims of behaviour for young persons (*Q*:
Is labor a curse or a blessing? *A*: Constant moderate labor
is the greatest of blessings).

'A stagnant, putrid pool'? Lincoln himself was to make
the most of his legend as a frontier lad, and sentimentalized
some of his childhood in jejune verse:

My childhood home I see again
And gladden with the view:
And still as mem'ries crowd my brain
There's sadness in it too.

He never learnt to relish the pioneering life, though, and
was never much interested in agricultural affairs – he said
he was taught how to work the land but not how to
enjoy doing it. He was never exactly ashamed of his
origins, and was not above politically exploiting them,
but he preferred to stay well clear. It was left to one of
his own admirers, many years later, to erect a headstone
above his poor mother's grave, in a clearing among the
Indiana woods (where she lies, by the way, not far from
a putative kinsman of hers, Joseph H. Morris). In adult
life he seldom visited even his amiable stepmother,
although for many years they both lived in the same
State, and he was always to be irritated by the whining
ineptitude of relatives. As for his father, Lincoln so dis-
liked him that he declined to visit his last bed of sickness,
contenting himself with a sanctimonious message to the
effect that our great, good and merciful Maker notes the
fall of a sparrow, numbers the hairs of our heads, and
will not forget the dying man who puts his trust in Him
. . . 'If we could meet now,' he wrote in declining to
visit the paternal deathbed, 'it is doubtful whether it
would not be more painful than pleasant.'

According to Dennis Hanks, a disreputable cousin
who lived with the Lincolns and in later years became a
kind of familiar, Abraham was obsessed with the Arabian
Nights stories, reading them over and over again. 'Them

stories is nothing but a pack of lies,' Dennis complained once. 'Mighty fine lies,' said Abraham, perhaps comparing the magic sunlit world of Scheherazade, Sinbad and the flying horse with the gloomy forest outside his own window, and the company he kept.

Three years at Sinking Spring, Kentucky, five more at the nearby Knob Creek Farm, another eleven at Little Pigeon Creek in Indiana – it was not until he was nineteen that Abraham Lincoln had a glimpse of life outside the backwoods. In 1828 he was invited to help a young boatman named Allan Gentry take a flatboat loaded with frontier produce to New Orleans, 1,200 miles down the immense river system of the American interior. The boat, a kind of cabined raft, was 50 or 60 feet long: lading bills of the time suggest that the cargo included pork and hams, corn meal, oats, beeswax, beans, poultry and possibly live cattle. When they got to New Orleans they would sell both the cargo and the flatboat, and come home by river-steamer.

They started from Rockport, Indiana, and that old port on the Ohio has never forgotten the event. The river is a mile wide there, and often runs very high, swirling past the town loaded with tree stumps and miscellaneous flotsam. Then the bank is squelchy beneath one's feet, the wind smells of damp and mud, and when a towboat strains against the stream towards Louisville you can hardly hear the heavy beat of its engines through the water's rush. From Rockport the river runs away to the west in an inexorably haughty manner, as though it means to flow to the other side of the world – as it very nearly does, for by combining with the even mightier Mississippi, its waters end up at last in the tropical Gulf of Mexico.

Beside the old river landing, below the bluffs of Rockport, a memorial stone remembers Lincoln's embarkation. Gentry the captain was at the long tiller aft, the mate Lincoln watched for snags and shallows forward, when they caught the stream downriver. In those days, when roads were scarce and often impassable, the western rivers were busy with the comings and goings of thousands of craft – paddle-steamers belching wood-smoke from their funnels, barges, skiffs, huge rafts and multitudinous flatboats. I doubt if anyone took much notice of Gentry and Lincoln as they pushed off – just two more young men on yet another flatboat. It was a fateful sailing nevertheless, for this first water-voyage was a metaphor of Lincoln's urge to get away from the cramped and arid narrative of his boyhood.

The rivers were the super-highways of his youth, the great escape routes, the contemporary equivalent of Kerouac's motorbike turnpikes. They gave him his first taste of life beyond the log cabin, as television might today, and they were his promise of freedom, as a university could have been. For a time he wanted to make a career as a professional river-man, and boats were always to play an important part in his life. Many an old tale lists his boyhood experiences on the rivers – how he earned his first dollars taking passengers to a steamer in mid-stream, how he worked as a ferryman on the Ohio, how he built his own boats and acted as a pilot on the Sangamon. He patented a device to enable river-steamers to lift themselves over shallows: it was US Patent No. 6,469, and there is a model of it still in the Smithsonian in Washington.

'Whenever I come this way,' said a passing lady exercising her dog, as I stood one day in contemplation at the Rockport landing-stage, 'I fancy Mr Lincoln out there on his boat. Can't you just see him there?' Of course I could – it's my trade! – but I suspect she and I saw different navigators on that flatboat. She saw Mr Lincoln in his stove-pipe hat, black suit and beard, perhaps with his shawl over his shoulders, but I saw the gangling young Abe in his reach-me-downs, cautiously poling a way through the snags as the eddy took them round the point. He always looks and feels like a river-man to me. He was a man of canny calculation, a man for the slow emergency, and the very sprawl of the American rivers suggest to me his own later presence, gawky but grand. Even in 1829, when he was not yet out of the boondocks, a great inchoate ambition was beginning to stir in him, and his first experience of the river system, his first sight of cosmopolitan New Orleans, doubtless gave him visions of the vast scale, power and meaning of America, and its limitless opportunities. Manifest Destiny; Monroe Doctrine; Go West, Young Man!; Sea to Shining Sea – all the old mantras of American pride stir in my own consciousness, even now, when I watch the great rivers go by.

The money Lincoln made from that first adventure into liberty had by law to be handed over to his feckless Dad. 'I know what it is to be a slave,' he said years later, and this is probably what he had in mind. I can well imagine

Thomas Lincoln claiming his cash, and even the young Abraham keeping something back on the sly. Who could blame him? Convention presents him as a paragon of truthfulness and square dealing, but it is hard to believe that, growing up in such a milieu, the boy was altogether immune to its mores.

So it is proper, I suppose, that around the Lincoln birthplace symptoms of the white trash society are still in evidence – one can hardly imagine the cabin at Sinking Spring transposed to some immaculate countryside of New England, or even to a stately tract of Old Virginia. Unbelievably obese families wander through the site, or peer into its eponymous spring, and just up the road there is one of those shambled settlements of trailers and scruffy shacks, with NO TRESPASSING warnings stuck on trees everywhere. I was there once at a time of local elections in Kentucky, and all over the place pasteboard notices on sticks invited the support of the electorate for one candidate or another – TROMBO FOR JAILER was one that seemed to me aesthetically apt.

But as for that log cabin itself, genuine or not, long ago Posterity laid its hands upon it, and did to it what it had already done to Abe Lincoln himself: apotheosized it. At one time entrepreneurs from Louisville hoped to make Lincoln Birthday Whiskey from the water of Sinking Spring, but the site was saved for a still higher destiny. In 1911 a patriotic association re-erected the cabin in a commanding position overlooking the spring, and surrounded it with a manicured park. The architect John Russell Pope was then commissioned to encase it within a large white classical temple, with Doric columns and chiselled inscriptions of inspiration, and a ceremonial staircase of fifty-six steps (one for each year of Lincoln's life). It was hoped that this noble sanctuary might dissuade young Americans from looking only to Europe for spiritual inspiration. It does rather suggest Ludwig of Bavaria's Valhalla above the Danube at Regensburg, then one of the prime destinations of cultural tourism, or even more appositely, the basilica at Assisi that immures within its vast marble spaces St Francis' original woodland chapel. National Park ladies guard the shrine at Sinking Spring, sporadically launching into educational monologues, and wondering matrons squeeze their way with difficulty around the cabin.

If the heaviest of the pilgrims have found those fifty-six steps too much for them, they may return to the Park Visitor Center by way of a more accommodating boardwalk, called the Pathway of a President. I am a foreign agnostic, though, trying to work out for myself the true nature of Abraham Lincoln, and I prefer to take the symbolical staircase – restraining myself, in deference to the National Park Service, from skipping down it whistling 'Yankee Doodle Dandy'.

Two

Out of the woods – a frontier shtetl - son of the people – no God? – M.
Owens and A. Rutledge – soldiering – birth of a lawyer – birth of a politician

In 1830 the Lincoln family finally emerged blinking, so
to speak, out of the Indiana forests into Illinois. They
were guided over the Wabash River, if we are to believe
the evidence of a memorial beside the river at Vincennes,
by a flying angel in the sky above. Parking their wagons
yet again, building themselves yet another cabin
(upgraded to floorboards by now, the second Mrs Lincoln
evidently having firmer views than the first), they settled
in Macon County near Decatur. This seems to me much
the happiest of their residences. The site is now a delightful clearing in the trees above the Sangamon River,
colourful in season with dogwood and butterflies, with
lush green grass where the Lincolns grew their crops,

and steps down to the river where Abraham once built himself a canoe. It makes me think of Torcello in the Venetian lagoon. When I peer through the trees that line its river bank, there in the sunshine extend the rich flatlands of Illinois, to my fancy just like the Adriatic shallows, with distant traffic passing silently to and fro like fishing boats on the horizon, and isolated white farms among their windbreaks so resembling little islands that I can almost see their reflections in the wheat fields. It is the prairie that faces me there, the start of the open West, and after the long haul along the Lincoln Heritage Trail, like Venice after a night flight it has the look of another world.

Here Abraham Lincoln, perhaps reading that landscape rather as I do, decided he had had enough of boyhood. He was no longer compulsorily indentured to his father. He was twenty-two years old, and free to do what he liked. He had spent too long, I would guess, shacked up with the inhabitants of the Lincoln log cabins – Thomas and Sarah Bush Johnston, Dennis Hanks, Elizabeth Johnston, John D. Johnston and Matilda Johnston, all hugger-mugger among the three-legged stools, spinning-wheels, cauldrons, quilts, spittoons, corn-cobs, animal hides, wooden toys, bunk beds, coon-skin hats and pumpkins that I imagine to have been the pioneering décor. He extracted himself from the comfortless and philistine congestion of it all, and never came back.

Instead, after a second flatboat trip to Louisiana, he settled at the village of New Salem, some 40 miles to the west, which was then one of the more promising young communities of Illinois. Its promise was false, as it happened, and in ten years or so New Salem more or less disappeared from the map: but we can see just what it was like in its heyday, when it contained about a hundred inhabitants living in a cluster of well-built log cabins, because in memorial to its most famous citizen it was reconstructed in the 1930s and renamed Lincoln's New Salem. By then only one of its original cabins was still standing, but they diligently rebuilt all the others, stocked the place with cows and horses, ploughed its fields and tilled its forgotten gardens once again, and re-created it just as it was, up in the woods above the Sangamon.

Inevitably it is really a folk museum – nobody actually lives there, and there is a McDonald's beside the Visitor Center, and a restaurant near by called Baby Bull's Café – but when I first walked into New Salem, early one autumn morning, I thought it rather like one of those wooden villages of Poland, or Lithuania, or western Russia, that one sees in the dim photographic backgrounds of pogroms. Nothing very terrible ever happened in New Salem, but it suggested to me all the same just such a close-knit, intense little entity bound together by the will to survive and to get on in the world against all hazards. The carding-mill and the stores, the blacksmith's, the tavern and the post office all stand stalwart enough along the unpaved village street, and the whole place is criss-crossed and enclosed by the zigzag fences of split oak logs that were a hallmark of the American frontier. The Sangamon has shifted since Lincoln's time, away from the bluff, but there is a reconstructed mill on its bank, and a landing-place for the pleasure boat that brings tourists here in the summer.

Downstream a grey mist often rises off a bend in the river, like a fog off the steppes.

Like those more fated settlements of Europe, New Salem was rich in characterful citizens, and was largely self-supporting. Compared with the straggly settlements of Indiana and Kentucky, it was a metropolis. It sent its own representative to the Illinois State legislature at Vandalia, to the south, and to the young Lincoln it offered liberation. A debating society flourished, newspapers were available, poker was played, horses were raced, brawls were frequently brawled. Visiting ministers often preached in New Salem, and there were educated people around, who possessed books and understood something of the world outside – almost the first such people Lincoln had got to know. Ambitious young entrepreneurs, a doctor, a lawyer, craftsmen of several kinds, a schoolmaster and a gang of adolescent louts all lived with their families close to one another, in houses of more or less equal consequence, on a post-coach route from Louisville. It was said that there was no such thing as a principal citizen in New Salem: everyone was a principal citizen there. Like those Jewish *shtetls* of eastern Europe, it was a tightly integrated society of heightened self-awareness.

Here Lincoln was on his own at last. Aware that he was out of the ordinary, already ambitious but gauche and uncertain, he could try himself out. He was, so he said, 'a piece of floating driftwood', and during his six years in New Salem he had a go at everything. Of course he worked on the river, for a start. In 1832 the steamboat *Talisman* sailed to New Salem from Cincinnati, by way of the Ohio, Mississippi and Sangamon rivers, in an attempt to open up a regular service with the Illinois frontier settlements. The excitement was wild. New Salem would be commercially transformed by direct connection with the east, and the river bank was hastily subdivided into lots for development. Lincoln was certainly caught up in the frenzy; but when it all went wrong, the river level fell, it was realized that the Sangamon could never handle big traffic and the ship had to make an ignominious withdrawal, he signed on as assistant pilot to see her safely out of the Sangamon again. The *Talisman* was burnt out a few months later (though today's New Salem pleasure boat is named after her): but if the enterprise had succeeded, Lincoln might well have fulfilled his adolescent hopes of a career on the river.

As it was, odd jobs in New Salem were easy to come by. He was the village postmaster for a time. He served with the volunteer militia. He learnt the craft of surveying. He was a partner in a general store, which went bankrupt and left him with debts that took years to pay off. He interested himself in politics and the law, and he still read a lot. He never finished a novel in his life, so he said, having failed like all too many of us to get through *Ivanhoe*; but we hear now of Aesop's Fables, *Pilgrim's Progress*, bits of Shakespeare, some Byron, some Milton and Gray's 'Elegy in a Country Churchyard'. As he once wrote:

> *Good boys who to their books apply*
> *Will all be great men by and by.*

Another huge body of folk tradition was to arise around the memory of Abraham at New Salem, some of it true, some apocryphal. Much of it concerned his status as a son of the people – it was always important to the Lincoln persona that he be thought of as 'everybody, grown a little taller'. In one of the most famous of the tales we read of him winning a wrestling bout against the toughest of the local louts, and thus gaining the approval of the obstreperous Clancy's Grove gang – who were not just your endearing village rascals, but thuggish enough to break the windows and smash the walls of people who crossed them. As postmaster he obligingly franked letters for friends with his official stamp, to save them the postage, and he is said to have once won a bet by drinking a whole barrel of whiskey while lying on his back (perhaps the origin of his later aversion to alcohol). He refereed cock-fights, he judged horse-races, perhaps he even brought himself to cheer with the rest down at the gander-pulling ground, where the youth of New Salem contested in the horseback game of decapitating live geese. He was taken to court when he failed to pay for a horse and tack he had bought ($57.86). And time and again we are told of his comic stories. Nobody could tell a comic story quite like Abe, and however often he told it, he still found it comical himself. He might be a bookworm and an oddball, but he was a practised slow teller of homespun jokes, occasionally scatological (probably the fart-and-turd kind), and in New Salem that clinched his acceptance as one of the boys. It was a gift he was always to retain, for my tastes the least appealing of his talents – a gift that still belabours Mid-Western conversations of a certain age, and has made the slow-talking elderly Middle Westerner with a twinkle in his eye one of the persons I least want to sit next to on a long-haul flight.

As I wandered one day around Lincoln's New Salem undertaking what I fondly call research, I came across such a man wearing a straw hat, sitting on the porch of one of the stores. 'How are you today?' said this man. 'Oh, I'm OK, I guess,' said I, falling politely into the language, but the man seemed affronted. 'OK? What d'ya mean, OK? Don't you know your alphabet? *P* comes after O, not K.' This reminded me of the old English music-hall dialogue between the delivery man and the housewife – 'What comes after S, missus?' 'T?' 'Thank you luv, I could just do with a cup' – but I laughed anyway, and the man removed his hat to wipe his brow. 'Ah well,' he said, 'it's a lovely day. It's the second happiest day of my life. Wanta know what the happiest day was? The day my divorce came through.'

I laughed dutifully again, and the man went on to tell me, as I feared he might, that Mr Lincoln himself loved such quips and funny stories. 'Did you know that?' Did I not! The books are full of Mr Lincoln's quips and funny stories. Later in life he was to use them formidably as political parables or smokescreens, or in therapeutic antidote to his own latent melancholy – 'to whistle down his sadness', one friend put it. Here at Salem, when he was in his twenties, they were generally jokes for joking's sake, usually taken from comic anthologies, seldom original inventions. What a bore the young Lincoln must have been, when he launched into anecdotal performance in his high-pitched voice! How one's jaw would have ached with the effort of appreciation! I excused myself from the man in the straw hat, afraid of being offered more examples, and took care to avoid any other derivative comics, during my visit to New Salem.

During his own time in the village Lincoln experienced many of the trials of young manhood, and some of them marked him for life. For one thing he apparently reached the conviction that there was no God. This is a common enough conviction nowadays, and was fashionable in Europe then. There were even a few free-thinkers in New Salem. Still, in an Illinois frontier village of the 1830s, when Baptists, Methodists and diverse evangelical sects competed for spiritual mastery, atheism was a risky thing to confess. Imagine the shock among the peripatetic ministers who rode around the frontier country then, preaching God's holy and immovable Word! Think of the affront to the log-cabin schoolteachers, doing their best to inculcate their charges with a proper sense of duty and divine mercy! Lincoln is said to have written a long essay on the subject at New Salem, but the manuscript has never been found, and although the rumour of his atheism dogged him for years, he never admitted it. The most he would say was that he was not a member of any organized church.

His parents were active church-goers, and old Thomas was actually a founder of the Pigeon Creek Baptist Church. But the Evanses of Bryn Gwyn had gravitated to Quakerism when they came to America, and Lincoln used to talk about Quaker roots: he sometimes addressed correspondents as 'Friend' – 'Friend Johnson', 'Friend Mary' – in the old Quaker manner. My guess is that his youthful Godlessness presently matured, as it often does, into agnosticism – perhaps he thought, as I do, that no honest man could really claim anything more. He was also subject to a profound half-pagan sense of mysticism, mixed up with the peasant superstitions of his childhood. Dreams and nightmares haunted him. He trusted in Fate and Providence, and eventually came to rely upon some invisible, intangible, unimaginable supernatural power presiding over all human fortunes – the solution of baffled philosophers down the ages. Attempts to portray him as an orthodox Christian of the time, spouting sanctimony and conventional piety, never did ring true. He some-times used the standard religious rhetoric ('our good, great and merciful Maker notes the fall of a sparrow'), but coming from him it sounded at best opportunist, at worst hypocritical. Religiosity never was his style. He used to say, quoting 'an old man of Indiana', that 'when I do good I feel good, when I do bad I feel bad, and that's my religion.'

Sexual challenges came to him at New Salem too. The young Lincoln was not at ease with women. He was at home with men of all kinds and ages, but women brought out the bumbling in him. In his boyhood, although he was close to his stepmother and his sister, he never seems to have played around much with the local girls, and at New Salem he even shied away from serving women in his store. As one woman was later to say of him, 'his peculiar manner and his general deportment would not be likely to fascinate a young girl.' His attitude neverthe-less seems to have been more feminist than macho. He

professed himself in favour of female suffrage, said he
was glad he wasn't born a woman because he could never
say no, and used to quote (and perhaps wrote) a jingle
decidedly sympathetic to the female condition:

> *Whatever spiteful fools may say*
> *Each jealous, ranting yelper,*
> *No woman ever went astray*
> *Without a man to help her.*

I would have guessed he was rather under-sexed, and
others declare him unilaterally gay, but Herndon wrote
that, on the contrary, he had difficulty repressing his
heterosexual passions – 'he could hardly keep his hands
off a woman.' Certainly in retrospect several women
claimed to have been courted by him: Miss Elizabeth
Wood, for instance, who said she declined his approaches
because of his large feet, or Miss Hannah Gentry who
thought he was too fond of onions. Perhaps the truth is
that he had bisexual instincts – and why not?

Anyway, at New Salem Lincoln allegedly had two
romantic encounters which were perhaps to affect him
for life. One was with a Mary Owens from Kentucky,
whose sister was a New Salem resident. An ample but
pleasant-looking young woman, she came on a visit to
the village, and when she went home again Lincoln
exchanged letters with her. He seems to have made a
vague suggestion of marriage but ended the exchange
with the valedictory throw-away 'If it suits you best
not to answer this, farewell. A long life and a merry
one attend you.' The marriage proposal petered out,

apparently ending with a refusal from Ms Owens, who married somebody else instead. The relationship was to be remembered, though, not because either party was greatly distressed by the end of it (Mary thought Lincoln 'deficient in those little links which make up a woman's happiness'), but because of the ham-handed and embarrassingly immature way in which he explained it away.

For when it was all over Lincoln described what had happened in a letter to a married woman friend that can still make one squirm. It was true, he said, that he had been somewhat in love with Mary Owens, sometimes hoping to marry her, sometimes resolving, as ambitious young men do, to stay clear of entanglements; but long before she refused him he had already regretted the proposal. What had turned him against it was Mary's physical appearance when he met her again after a separation: 'I knew she was oversize, but now she appeared a fair match for Falstaff . . . now as I beheld her I could not for my life avoid thinking of my mother; and this not from her withered features – for her skin was too full of fat to permit of it contracting into wrinkles – but from her want of teeth and weather-beaten appearance in general . . .' These were the responses, he said, that resolved him to get out of his 'scrape'; and although it is true he wrote this letter on April Fool's Day, and was perhaps trying partly to amuse, and anyway did not mention Mary Owens by name, I dare say when he grew older it came back to him, now and then, to make him squirm, too.

Far more tender and suitable to the Lincoln myth is the tale of Ann Rutledge, with whom he was supposed to have had a sad, passionate and unfulfilled affair during his New Salem years – the one true love of his life, it has often been said. The story was first told to a receptive public, soon after Lincoln's death, by William Herndon, who had lived in New Salem too, and had supposedly picked it up from neighbours and acquaintances. It has been variously believed and discounted ever since – believed by wishful romantics, discounted by sceptical historians. Ann, the daughter of an innkeeper, was engaged to a New Yorker then resident in the village, who called himself John McNeil. He presently admitted that this was a pseudonym, assumed because his parents disapproved of his emigration to the West, and he announced that he was returning to New York to mollify them. He would be back, he told Ann, and a couple of letters did arrive before he faded for ever out of life and legend. In the mean time the young Abe, a temporary lodger at the Rutledge inn, fell hopelessly in love with Ann, and she with him. They walked together, we are told, they read books together, they talked about everything as lovers do (even about atheism, I dare say, for Ann Rutledge was an intelligent girl who hoped for a university education). One thing they did not do, I think we can assume, was sleep together: holding hands in the moonlight, reciting maudlin poetry to each other, was probably the nearest they got to orgasm.

It is a pathetic fable – Ann still betrothed to her vanished Easterner, Abraham head over heels for the first time in his life! When the Rutledge family moved to the nearby settlement of Petersburg, so Herndon's inform-ants told him, Abraham walked over there night and day to see his beloved. The tale caught the heart-strings of simple Americans, and sentimentalists like me have preferred to trust in it ever since. What gave the story its only possible ending was Ann's death at the age of twenty-two, probably from cholera. Lincoln was then twenty-six, and we are told that he was never the same again. His long spells of depression, his customary tristesse, the sad look in his eyes that everyone was to notice – all these, Herndon maintained, sprang from his cruel loss, and Ann Rutledge was long commemorated in the popular mind as Lincoln's lifelong love.

Novelists, poets, playwrights, film-makers and forgers in every degree of subtlety and sloppiness have celebrated her memory since Herndon first introduced her to the world. Pilgrims for ever after have visited her supposed grave in the cemetery above the neighbouring village of Petersburg. Lincoln himself, they say, often went there, and told somebody that the thought of snows and rains falling on it 'filled him with indescribable grief'. I find it a touching little burial place, because as a matter of fact nobody is quite sure that Ann is really buried there, and because the epitaph on the headstone was written by one of Lincoln's few debunkers, the local poet Edgar Lee Masters:

> *I am Ann Rutledge who sleeps beneath these weeds*
> *Beloved in life of Abraham Lincoln,*
> *Wedded to him, not through union,*
> *But through separation.*
> *Bloom forever, O Republic,*
> *From the dust of my bosom!*

At New Salem Lincoln also learnt to live as a man among men. When he was twenty-three a small war broke out in the West. The Sauk and Fox Indian tribes had been driven from their ancestral lands in Illinois to the western side of the Mississippi, and were obliged to agree that they would never return 'to their usual place of residence, nor any part of their old hunting grounds . . .' In 1832 their venerable chieftain Black Hawk, faced with starvation among his people, decided to return anyway, and led them back over the river into Illinois. Volunteers were called for to deal with this 'aggression', and times being hard for Lincoln at that moment, he joined Colonel Thompson's Regiment of Mounted Volunteers. In those days American citizen soldiers elected their own officers, and Lincoln was chosen by his comrades to be captain of his company – always to be one of his proudest memories, just as William Gladstone got his greatest sense of achievement from his election to the Eton schoolboy society called 'Pop'.

Brought up to the frontier life, Lincoln took soldiering as it came. He never fired a shot against the Indians, but he roughed it in the field and learnt some of the elementary military arts, including improvisation: it always amused him to recall that when he forgot the correct commands to get the marching men of his column through a narrow gate, he ordered them to break ranks and fall in again on the other side of it. At the river-port of Beardstown, on the Illinois River some 20 miles from New Salem, he fought a famous wrestling match against the captain of another company, and there, too, he apparently lost his virginity to a local whore. It was probably his first sexual intercourse, and no more than just a display of soldierly bravado – how many millions of young men have visited their first prostitute, and often their last, in uniform? As one of his fellow soldiers said, they all went to brothels 'purely for fun – devilment – nothing else'. Lincoln rather thought he had caught syphilis from the girl, but that was probably nervous self-delusion – he was always rather a hypochondriac (although when he spoke about bouts of 'hypo' he was referring to his chronic melancholy).

He later made fun of his military experiences, but actually he was rather proud of them. When his first tour of duty was over he enlisted for another, and he would be gratified to see the image of himself as a soldier which stands beside his tomb at Springfield today – such a fine, lean, self-confident figure of a horseman, so easy in the saddle, with his slouch hat turned up at the brim like a Boer commando and his long frontiersman's rifle under his arm. The sculptor Fred M. Torrey created this heroic image, but I dare say a truer glimpse of Lincoln the soldier is provided by a remark from one of his more perceptive comrades. Abe always got on well with his men, said this memoirist, although they were a tough and independent crew, not fond of discipline. 'He was doubtless looking a long away ahead, when both their friendship and respect would be of avail.'

For by now he was clearly ambitious for something or other – 'floating driftwood' perhaps, but floating to a gradually revealed purpose. At New Salem Lincoln the lawyer was born, and he was licensed to practise while he was living there. The folklore says he learnt his law from a copy of Sir

William Blackstone's *Commentaries on the Laws of England*, 1769, which he found at the bottom of a barrel of junk. Actually he often walked from New Salem to Springfield, a nearby and rather larger town, to borrow law books, and he had some elementary tuition from a local schoolmaster, the happily christened Mentor Graham.

I can well believe the stories that say he studied his law books all day long – *studying*, not just *reading*, he used to remonstrate – propping them up beside him as he served in the store, lying flat on his back barefoot, with a book like a sunshade above him, deep in them I do not doubt while he sat in the privy, reading them aloud as he trudged the 20 miles there and back from Springfield. It was a surprising sight to simpler citizens of New Salem, who tended to think of him, as his father had, as a bit of a loafer. 'What are you studyin', Abe?' inquired a farmer who found him deep in a book on top of a woodpile. 'Studyin' law.' 'Great God Almighty,' was all the farmer could think of replying.

Asked by a tyro in later years what was required to become a lawyer, Lincoln replied, 'Work and work – the secret of success in law is work.' But it was easy for him to say, because the work was clearly a pleasure for him, and the law itself never lost its fascination. It suited his temperament. Especially when he was young his mind worked best by reasoning, abetted by guile. He would innocuously give away six points, so one of his opponents said, in order to win on the seventh. He liked the symmetry of a logical argument, the order of a syllogism – so akin to a parable – but he also had a gift for the sudden pounce that clinched an argument.

The most popularly famous demonstration of this last ability was to happen years later at Beardstown, 'the friendliest little city on the Illinois river', as its publicity people like to say nowadays, the Watermelon Capital of the Nation. Beardstown is everyone's idea of a small home town of the Middle West. It has a pleasant green square with a memorial gun in it, and a viewing platform on the river where you can watch the tows sail by, and above the baseball diamond in the public park people sit on the river levee to watch the game over beers and Diet Cokes. It is the kind of place where total strangers wave you good morning out of pick-up trucks, or tell you without your asking just where they were on the day the towboat ran into the levee back in 1972.

Lincoln knew Beardstown well. To Beardstown he helped pilot the poor *Talisman* on her ignominious retreat from New Salem. At Beardstown, in that public park, he wrestled his rival company commander. Somewhere in Beardstown he slept with his whore. And in the court-house beside Beardstown's square he pulled off his celebrated legal coup. The building functions as a court to this day, but now also houses the town museum and the City Hall, and in the city clerk's office you can buy buckets of frozen gourmet cookie dough made by local church members. It was a Sunday when I turned up there myself, and only a policewoman in her cubicle beside the back door was on duty. She offered me the run of the building – 'take your time, have fun' – but as the only visitor of the morning I walked quickly past the cookie dough, briskly through the museum, straight by

the chamber of Judge Fred W. Reither into the courtroom itself.

This is exactly like a country courtroom in an old film,
with big windows looking out on the square, polished
wooden benches, and photographs of mayors, judges and
sheriffs on its walls. I thought it marvellously evocative,
full of lively shades, so I sat myself in Judge Reither's
swivel chair, at his high desk above the benches, and
supposed myself to be inviting Mr Lincoln to present his
case. There and then he unfolded his sinewy frame below
me, and started talking very loud and penetratingly in
his high tenor. 'Kindly lower your voice, Mr Lincoln,'
I heard myself interrupting, and off the top of my head
I could hear him reply: 'My apologies, Judge, but as I
was saying, the case in hand reminds me of the story of
the farmer and his blind duck . . .'

I skipped a little in my mind then, for I imagined the
tale going on and on rather; but I will say this for Abe's
stories, that they were seldom off the point, and in fact
he won this particular case in true Perry Mason style. He
demonstrated that an allegedly moonlit murder could
not have been witnessed because there was no moon
that night – and proved the point by flourishing before
the jury's eyes an almanac for the month. He won hands
down, and he ended his argument (or so I liked to
imagine) with a conclusive aside to me – 'which is, Judge,
as you will doubtless have appreciated, very much what
the farmer argued in relation to the duck and its broken
egg . . .' We all laughed, me and my vivacious ghosts,
there in the empty courtroom that Sunday morning: and
nobody laughed louder than young 'Duff' Armstrong,

formerly of the Clancy's Grove mob, saved from the gallows in the Great Almanac Trial and thus improbably immortalized. Lincoln himself, to commemorate the event, went around the corner to Abraham Byer's Photographic Studio, 101 State Street, and had his picture taken in a white suit that looks rather too big for him.

Finally and most fatefully at New Salem, in that small frontier village in its clearing above the woods, Abraham Lincoln began his career as a politician. His very first political manifesto appeared in the Springfield newspaper, the *Sangamo Journal*, on 15 March 1832, and ended with this declaration: 'Every man is said to have his peculiar ambition. Whether it be true or not, I can say, for one, that I have no other so great as that of being truly esteemed by my fellow men, by making myself worthy of their aim. How far I shall succeed in gratifying this ambition, is yet to be developed. I am young and unknown to many of you. I was born and have ever remained in the most humble walks of life. I have no wealthy relations to commend me . . . If the good people in their wisdom shall see fit to keep me in the background, I have been too familiar with disappointment to be very much chagrined.'

He had made his first political speech two years before at Decatur. During a political meeting outside Renshaw's Store, in the middle of the little town, he was urged to speak – as everyone knew, young Abe could talk the back legs off a mule. Fresh as he was from his original flatboat experience, he obliged with an unexpected dissertation about the economic potential of local river navigation, and the occasion is remembered still by a statue in Decatur's Lincoln Square (it shows him standing barefoot and shirt-sleeved on the sawn-down stump of a tree, which is indeed the original meaning of stump-speaking). The experience seems to have fired him. Within two years he was offering himself as representative for New Salem in the State Assembly at Vandalia, with the manifesto that appeared in the *Sangamo Journal*. In many ways it was like the statement of a candidate for a student union somewhere. Again he stressed the importance of river development, besides some more obviously populist matters like reducing interest rates and promoting education – 'offering the people,' as he said in true student-union humbuggery, 'the advantages and satis-faction to be derived from all being able to read the Scriptures, and other works of both a religious and moral nature for themselves.' But those concluding lines of his newspaper credo were something else – a sign that he had already grasped the political power of emotion. Pathos and humility would always serve him as political tools, together with humour and a pragmatic species of simplicity.

In 1832 these techniques in embryo evidently left *some* dry eyes in the house, because he lost his first election. He won next time round, though, borrowed $200 from one of his voters to buy a new suit, and thus began his political apprenticeship at Vandalia, 75 miles away (which meant three days in a stage-coach). Even by the standards of the West in the 1830s, this was an extraordinary little place. It was hardly more than another village of log cabins, on a bluff above the Kaskaskia River, with streets of dust and mud. Its Capitol building was only four years old but was falling down already. The Vandalia Inn, where Lincoln lodged during Legislative sessions, was no more than a country tavern. Yet this unprepossessing and unhealthy hamlet, on the edge of a swamp, seethed with all the intrigue, passion, rivalry, violence, mayhem and excitement of nineteenth-century American politics. Caucuses struck secret deals, demagogues made accusations, legislators indulged in public fisticuffs and the *Vandalia Free Press* observed everything with a jaundiced eye from its log-cabin office.

It was a fine school for a political tyro. For the time being Lincoln turned his back on the law and threw himself into his second calling. During his time in Vandalia – about a year's residence there in aggregate – he learnt a lot about balancing power, swapping privileges, cliques, deals and patronage. He joined the Whig Party, in opposition to the Democrats, because it shared his own preferences for a national banking system, protective tariffs and material development at federal expense: and he supported an extravagant Improvement Plan for Illinois, including the building of railroads in all corners of the State, making every single river navigable, and building a canal to link the Illinois River with Lake Michigan. He became a leading member of the delegation from Sangamon County, with two State Senators and seven Representatives who were all Whigs, too. They were known as the Long Nine, because they were all over six feet tall, and their chief achievement during Lincoln's two sessions in the Legislature was to get the capital transferred from Vandalia to the centre of their own constituency, Springfield.

The understandably embittered *Free Press*, about to be reduced from a metropolitan newspaper to a village rag, alleged that this was arranged by an exchange of favours on Lincoln's part: notably his backing for the madly impracticable and eventually disastrous Improvement Plan. The paper saw it as cynical opportunism. This was Lincoln's first experience of Press hostility, and for the first time too he felt the sting of opposition abuse – 'a coarse and vulgar fellow', Democrats called him, 'low and obscene'. Never mind, it was all part of the learning process. The Long Nine celebrated their victory with a banquet at Ebenezer Capps's tavern in Vandalia, where they got through eighty-one bottles of champagne.

Lincoln soon became, as everyone recognized, a highly motivated politician, and his style was carefully fashioned. It was a deceptively easy, laid-back style: his native Kentucky style, perhaps, if we are to take the word of the contemporary writer Harriet Beecher Stowe, who said your true Kentuckian wore his hat at all times, tumbled himself about, put his heels on the tops of chairs and mantelpieces 'and is altogether the frankest, easiest, most jovial creature living'.

Frank, easy and jovial is certainly how Abraham Lincoln presented himself to the voters. He was never like one of your young zealots of the next century, urgently propagating their callow ideologies – Mrs Thatcher's disciples of the British Young Conservatives, or clone-like interns of the White House. The political manner of his maturity is easily recognizable in 1832, like his physique, and in the countryside around New Salem I can still easily see his gaunt figure on the stump. He was twenty-three years old then, odd and ungainly still, with his huge feet and long neck, 6 foot 4 inches tall and skinny. He wore a straw hat in those days – a hat, Mrs Beecher Stowe tells us, was a characteristic emblem of a Kentucky man's sovereignty. The sleeves of his jacket were too short, and his off-white flax trousers reached no further than his ankles. He spoke at the hustings in the slow, irrepressible high-pitched cadences we heard in the courtroom at Beardstown, occasionally 'breaking off for repairs', we are told, 'before finishing a sentence'.

There he goes now, unmistakeable, shaking hands easily with men, self-consciously with women – telling a comical story here and there – sometimes intervening with his long muscular arms when a scuffle breaks out at a meeting, sometimes seizing a hoe to demonstrate that he is as genuine a working man as anyone else. It is a striking style, by no means as naïve as it looks. At home in Britain I once had a guest from the prairies who, when we passed men working in a field, digging a ditch or hedging, would leap from the car to show them a better way to do it, not for a moment noticing their condescending amusement. Lincoln would never have made that mistake. He was at once deliberate and sensitive in all things, and just as he had worked out his legal career sitting with his Blackstone's on the woodpile, so he was already devising an overt shape for his politics. 'My politics are short and sweet,' he said, keeping his fingers crossed I hope, 'like the old woman's dance.'

He had worked out a character for himself, too. It is

often said that Lincoln was remarkable because he was constantly developing – not just maturing, but evolving in a Darwinian sense, to meet the demands of his times. His years at New Salem represented a dramatic acceleration of the process. He went there almost totally inexperienced in life. He left the village, if we are to believe all the stories, scarred by love, mortified by bankruptcy, hardened by soldiering, tutored in law, blooded into politics, religiously independent, streetwise and sex-initiated. He went to New Salem a raw boy out of the backwoods, he left it a lawyer, a State legislator and consciously a man for a' that (for he already knew much of Robbie Burns by heart, according to his panegyrists, and had adopted the Scotsman's braw and canny populism).

Three

To Springfield – 'a thing of state' – tangled courtship – family life – the law – 'Hi Judge' – on slavery – into battle – on the mound – President-elect – 'she's got what she wanted'

When the time came to move on, in 1837, Lincoln packed his entire possessions in a couple of saddle-bags and rode a borrowed horse along the river to Springfield – very soon to become, thanks so largely to his own machinations, the new capital of Illinois. I went to this town for the first time on the Amtrak train called the Ann Rutledge, which stops there on its daily way from Chicago to Kansas City.

For my purpose it was the only way to go: quite apart from the name of the train, it was the railroad, after all, that had enabled these prairies to grow rich, and made it possible for Springfield itself, situated more or less in

the middle of nowhere, to become the capital of Illinois
– to this day, with its 106,000 inhabitants, the political
superior of Chicago up the line. For many of us foreigners
the American prairies have always seemed less an actual
place than a geographical notion – a sprawling and unen-
ticing plain, sometimes icy-cold, sometimes appallingly
hot, over which combine harvesters grind their way
through illimitable wheatfields, and in which very slow-
speaking raconteurs of the New Salem school swap
laborious pleasantries in all-too-likely-teetotal counties.
I needed to match the truth against the fancy.

At first the fancy seemed to win. It was November
when I made the journey, and Amtrak itself would not
claim that at that time of the year there is much excitement
to be seen through the windows of the Ann Rutledge.
The industrial towns we passed through reminded me
of Albania, so run-down were their rail-side factories
and warehouses, and in the grey light the prairie itself,
speckled with farmhouses and windbreaks, no longer
suggested to me the Venetian lagoon, but was more like
some stretch of wartime ocean, in which the masts and
superstructures of sunken ships protruded here and there
from the swell.

Springfield seemed hardly more inspiriting, when we
pulled in just before dusk. It was a public holiday, and
the town was half empty. The Illinois Legislature was
not in session, the Governor was out of town and at the
Hilton Hotel I appeared to be the only guest. I found a
clutch of tourist publicity material in my room on the
twenty-second floor, and tried to identify, in the vast
melancholy expanse outside my window, some of the

sites it recommended. Could I see, for example, the site of the Old Tyme Tractor Show at Hillsboro, or the Two-Storey Train Depot Museum at Greenup, or Taylorville, where Kay the Circus Elephant is buried – only the second elephant, so my brochure winningly told me, to die in Illinois?

But a veil of mist and cloud lay over the prairie, and if these varied marvels were ever visible from the Hilton Hotel, they were out of sight that day. On the other hand I could make out, close beneath the lee of the skyscraper, a little cluster of clapboard houses identified on my map as 'Mr Lincoln's Neighborhood'. I hastened down there at once – down my twenty-two floors in the echoing elevator – past the municipal garage on 7th Street and the First Presbyterian Church on the corner – first on the left and lo! all my despondency vanished.

The streets might be deserted, the vapours lay low, the restaurants were closed, the doors of the First Presbyterian Church were locked, but there before me stood one of the best-known and best-loved houses in all America: at 8th Street and Jackson, Springfield, Illinois, the only house that Abraham Lincoln ever owned, faintly glowing through the dusk with night-lights and charisma. From that moment I saw Springfield through new eyes, and all the symptoms of its prairie origins, the very clamour of the starlings around the Old Capitol building, were charged for me with allegory.

There are at least fourteen Springfields in the United States, besides three in Canada and one each in Kenya and New Zealand, but Abraham Lincoln made Springfield,

Illinois, infinitely more famous than any of the others. It had been founded in 1821, and physically it was still an unlovely little town when he moved in. Nowadays the wailing of train whistles sounds there all through the night, but in 1837 the nearest railway was still miles away, and in winter the country roads were so deep in mire, floods or snow that the place was more or less isolated. I imagine this helped to give it a strong sense of corporate identity, but it clearly did little for its allure.

About 1,500 people lived in Springfield then. The streets were unpaved and unlighted, the mud was some-times knee-deep, the buildings were dowdy red-brick, pigs wallowed in mud holes, litter filled the gutters and brothels flourished. In summer the town was full of stinks and flies. Nevertheless it was an outpost of relative civilization on the threshold of the comfortless West. There were shops and hotels and restaurants, and plenty of churches. Concerts and lectures were popular, theatrical companies, circuses and travelling menageries came visiting from time to time, and sometimes national celeb-rities were fêted as civic guests – ex-President van Buren, for instance, who was met outside the town by a cortège of principal citizens, rather as contemporary chancellors of Oxford University were greeted at the city limits by horseback dons.

Most of Springfield's citizens were white Anglo-Saxons, born in America, but there were some black people in Springfield, some Germans and Irish, and often there came straggling through town, perhaps to bivouac for the night in the main square, a wagon-train of emi-grants on their way to the far West. Eight hundred

Mormons, in sixty-seven wagons, passed through Spring-field one day in 1837, on their way to their Promised Land in Utah; two weeks later 800 Pottawatomie Indians, mostly on horseback, followed them in more reluctant migration – they were being forcibly relocated west of the Mississippi; and in 1846 Springfield waved *bon voyage* to the fated hopefuls of the Donner Pass party, the last of whom were all too soon to eat each other's corpses in a final extremity of starvation in the Rocky Mountains.

Springfield was already a highly political place. When Lincoln arrived in town they were hard at it completing a brand-new State House, in the centre of the town's main square, in readiness for their first Legislative session in 1840, but the rivalries of Whigs and Democrats had long been reverberating anyway. Sundry party intrigues enlivened the local gossip, and minuscule newspapers were constantly at each other's throats. Behind this political activity lay a self-conscious culture. Many of the town's posher citizens had moved there from the more developed parts of Kentucky, and Society with a capital S already existed, enjoyed its rounds of balls, tea parties and political soirées, and was beginning to build itself portentous houses with balconies and *porte-cochères*. Some remarkable young politicos frequented these circles, including numbers of future Congressmen, and the Springfield elect was proud too of its distinguished public forebears, some perhaps more authentic than others.

Lincoln, arriving on his borrowed horse from New Salem, and setting up as junior partner in a legal practice, felt out of things at first. He reported to Mary Owens that it was not much fun being poor in Springfield, where there was 'a great deal of flourishing about in carriages', and said he had never been lonelier in his life. Yet in the end he made the place. Who in the outside world knows anything about Lansing, the capital of Michigan, or South Dakota's Pierre, or Tallahassee, Florida? Mention Springfield, Illinois, though, and instantly everyone thinks of Lincoln. His connection with the town was to give it lustre ever after. It was the only town he ever called home.

Naturally, Springfield, a particularly agreeable city now, never lets you forget that he was the most famous of all its citizens. There are Abe Lincoln markers all over the place, an Abe Lincoln Garage, an Abe Lincoln hairdresser, Lincoln's law office and an emaciated statue of Lincoln, unveiled by Lord Charnwood in 1918, centre-stage outside the State Capitol. There is also the tomb where they buried him in the end, a prodigy of symbolism and writhing martial sculpture beneath a towering obelisk – bronze battle-flags, drums, brandished swords, batteries of artillery of course, terrified rearing horses, beards, drummer boys, sailors with telescopes and heroically dying soldiers. Jets from a nearby National Guard airfield often fly overhead, and in front of it all is a bust of Lincoln whose nose has been so polished by the fingers of superstitious pilgrims that you can see it shining from far across the cemetery, like the luminous nose of the Dong.

One of the most famous of all Lincoln poems, by the local poet Vachel Lindsay, imagines his ghost roaming the streets of Springfield:

It is portentous and a thing of state
That here at midnight, in our little town,
A mourning figure walks and will not rest.
Near the old courthouse, pacing up and down

Or by his homestead, or in shadowed yards
He lingers where his children used to play.
Or in the market on the well-worn stones
He stalks until the dawn-stars burn away.

It reminds me of Matthew Arnold's 'Scholar-Gipsy' (*in hat of antique shape, and cloak of grey*), and has the same effect upon me: for just as I can always see the Scholar, when my eye travels down to Oxford's towers from Bagley Wood, so I found I could summon Lincoln's presence anywhere in Springfield. If I bumped into a jolly, talkative lawyer, I saw him as just the kind of partner Lincoln would have had. When I encountered a folksy philosopher, I imagined the two of them outdoing each other in aphorism. I saw Abe Lincoln taking his beaver hat into James Haley's on 6th Street, where Hats are still Cleaned and Blocked, and popping into Downtown News and Books for the day's *Journal-Register*, which has his portrait on its masthead. At the Capitol Caffe one day I introduced myself to the assembled Poets' and Writers' Literary Forum, a most hospitable crew, and there was old Abe disentangling his long limbs to greet me, holding an ode of his own. At Maldaner's restaurant over the way, which is almost old enough to remember him *in corpore*, so to speak, I swear I heard him laughing with a bunch of cronies behind the swing doors of the bar.

It would not be surprising if Lincoln's phantom really did walk the streets of Springfield, because it meant so much more to him than any other place. If Lincoln made Springfield, Springfield certainly made Lincoln too. There he succeeded in law, became famous in politics, married his only wife, became a father and lost a son. There he reconciled himself to his flaws, honed his virtues, and endured such emotional challenges that he probably nearly went off his head, and certainly suffered some kind of mental breakdown. His time in Springfield was not an abrupt evolutionary progress, like his time in New Salem, but twenty-four such years might well bring back a man's ghost to walk the shadowed yards.

Lincoln was well known in Springfield even before he went to live in the town, if only because of his part in moving the capital there. He was not easily welcomed into Society, though. He had no money, for a start – he was still paying off debts from the bankruptcy in New Salem. Besides, he was such a particularly idiosyncratic young man. He was obviously clever, but fresh from the log cabins at twenty-eight he presented a gauche and awkward figure – poor, lean and lank was his self-description. He was lop-sided, his left shoulder being higher than his right. There was a slight cast in his left eye, caused by a kick from a horse. His beardless face was pinched. His complexion was sallow. He had cauliflower ears and a mole on his right cheek. His feet were flat and enormous. His voice was high-pitched, his accent bucolic Indiana. His arms seemed too long for his body and his walk was graceless – as though he needed oiling, Herndon said.

At first acquaintance he certainly did not seem a promising recruit for the Springfield élite. He was still uneasy with women of style and he dressed with decided inelegance: trousers and sleeves too short for him, heavy farm boots on his feet, cravats habitually askew and as often as not odd socks. He was too tall for drawing-rooms, the wrong shape for love-seats. What self-respecting hostess, directly descended from the *highest* echelons of Kentucky society, would welcome such a guest to her drawing-room? Yet such was his strange allure that even some of Springfield's snootiest hostesses recognized him as somebody special, out of the usual run, somebody to be cultivated after all: and so it happened that surprisingly soon, having presumably recovered from the Rutledge and Owens entanglements, Lincoln got to know one of the most self-consciously upper-crust young women in town.

Mary Ann Todd came from a family in Lexington, Kentucky, which considered itself aristocratic, and was certainly a long way from white trash. It wildly claimed to trace its ancestry back to the sixth century, and boasted any number of generals, governors and assorted bigwigs in its pedigree. The Todds had flourished in Lexington partly in commerce, partly in law, and possessed several handsome houses and numbers of slaves. They thought very highly of themselves, and none more highly than Mary Ann. Plump but prepossessing, self-opinionated and quick-witted, by the female standards of the day she was well educated – the best schools in Lexington had taught her, and she played the piano, and spoke French, and had most of the accomplishments thought essential for ladylike and marriageable behaviour, besides being fashionably subject to the vapours. She had come to Springfield to join her elder sister Elizabeth, whose husband Ninian Edwards was a prominent local toff, and she lived with them in their swanky house in the quarter of the town nicknamed 'Aristocracy Hill'. There in 1839 she met Abraham Lincoln, who was ten years her senior and already an active member of the new State Assembly in Springfield, and they were presently engaged to be married.

It was a tangled courtship. If Lincoln was, on the face of things, not much of a match for Mary, Mary was hardly an obvious mate for Lincoln. Physically they were almost ludicrously mismatched: the man so elongated, craggy and ill-dressed, the woman very short, almost fat, and preposterously bestowed with frills and ribbons. I suspect both approached marriage with an eye to the main chance. Both were ambitious. Mary, always mindful of her family glories, astutely realized that the young hick Lincoln would go far: Lincoln, with his mind on political advancement, saw advantages in Mary's wide and influential connections – and for that matter, in being married at all.

Undoubtedly Abraham soon became fond of Mary, though – so fond, that when in 1841 they parted company he fell into one of the profound clinical depressions which were to plague him all his life. He called 1841 'that fateful year', and in an urge to get away from Springfield he even angled unsuccessfully for a job as United States Chargé d'Affaires in Bogotá, Colombia, a desperate expedient indeed. He was suffering a breakdown. For weeks, we are told, he moped around the town doing nothing in particular, and it was now that his inborn taste for things gloomy and dejected caught hold of him. He grew to love the sadder parts of Shakespeare, concerning the deaths of kings or the shattering of illusions, and he became obsessed with a lyric by the Scottish poet William Knox, who had died sixteen years before, so the British *Dictionary of National Biography* tells me, because 'his convivial habits undermined his health'.

Lincoln had read 'Mortality' in a newspaper some-where, and its mournful themes and rhythms were to remain part of his mental repertoire all his life – a sort of leitmotif. 'Oh why should the spirit of mortal be proud,' asked this lugubrious composition, when everyone was going to die in the end?

> *'Tis the twink of an eye, 'tis the draught of a breath,*
> *From the blossom of health to the paleness of death,*
> *From the gilded salon to the bier and the shroud –*
> *Oh why should the spirit of mortal be proud!*

'I would give all I am worth,' Lincoln said, 'to be able to write so fine a piece,' and it certainly expressed his own emotions then. He was, he said, the most miserable man alive. 'If what I feel were equally distributed to the whole human family, there would not be one cheerful face on the earth. Whether I shall ever be better I cannot tell; I awfully forebode I shall not.'

Many reasons have been suggested for Lincoln's famous melancholy. Herndon put it down to the Ann Rutledge tragedy; others have suggested suppressed sexual urges, or chronic constipation. I think it was the long accretion of sadnesses in his life, beginning with his childhood losses, culminating in two causes of despondency in Springfield: first the split with Mary Todd, then their reconciliation.

For they were married after all in 1842; and although the couple were to be always loyal and essentially loving to each other, it seems to me that much of their life together was nightmare. Mary Todd turned out to be mentally unstable – those vaporous turns of hers were probably disturbances of the brain. She was also of dubious honesty and a frightful nagger. For his part Lincoln, I dare say, always wondered if he had taken the right sexual path. The wedding itself, *chez* Edwards, was hardly joyous. James H. Matheny, the best man, who was conscripted only on the wedding morning, thought the bridegroom looked and acted as though he were going to the slaughter, and when a small boy came across Lincoln all dressed up for the ceremony, and asked him where he was off to, he is supposed to have replied morosely, 'To hell, I suppose.' No Lincolns, Johnstons or Hankses were invited, perhaps to spare the feelings of the bride and her family – even Herndon characterized the Hankses as 'the lowest of the low', so they would not have pleased the fastidious Todds. 'Nothing new here,' the bridegroom wrote a week later to a friend of his, 'except my marrying, which is to me a matter of profound wonder.'

To begin with the couple lived in second-floor rooms at the modest Globe Tavern on Adams Street (along the road from the Hilton and almost opposite Abe Lincoln's

Hairdressing Shop). Mary must have thought it slumming rather, but in the second year of their marriage they moved into that house on 8th and Jackson. It was small and fairly mean when they bought it, but later they did it up to some degree of elegance – restored in the Greek Revival style, and painted chocolate brown with dark green shutters. This was more like it! The house has long been sanitized for the tourists by guardian nannies of the National Park Service, together with the adjacent streets of Mr Lincoln's Neighborhood ('Please exercise caution when walking within this restored 19th-century environment'), and is a pleasant two-storey frame building with four bedrooms and some outbuildings, its front door opening directly upon the street. Parties of tourists go round all day every day, jollied along in an educational way by uniformed guides, and there are booklets to tell you all about the neighbourhood, who lived next door to the Lincolns, down the street, across the lane, how well integrated the family was into the life of the town. It was a well-behaved middle-class district, a few hundred yards from the State House, three blocks from open country, not aspiring to the splendours of Aristocracy Hill, but just the place for an up-and-coming young citizen with good connections. Here Mary Todd Lincoln gave birth to four children – Robert in 1843, Eddie in 1846, Willie in 1850, and Thomas, born in 1853, slow, slightly handicapped in speech and always known as Tad, as in Tadpole. They were brought up on the principle that children could do no wrong.

It all sounds fine. The house has a happy air, and the Lincolns entertained generously and lived comfortably enough, with a servant or two to look after them, milk from the cow in the back shed, and plenty of the venison and wild game that abounded in the Illinois countryside. Lincoln himself was never much interested in food, did not smoke and was teetotal by now, but he could be an entertaining host and was a kind paterfamilias, skilful with a carving knife and always indulgent to bad manners from the children. I thought of their family table when I read the recipe for a thanksgiving dinner proposed by a pupil at Springfield elementary school in 1997: 'Go out in the woods and make sure if you see a turkey, shoot it. Take it home and get all the bones out. Skin it. Stuff a wishbone inside. Cook it for 30 minutes at four degrees. Say your dinner prayer. Pass out forks. Start chumping.'

But when I walk these streets nevertheless, looking out for Lincoln's ghost and exercising caution, I sense discordances. Lincoln was in some ways a disconcerting neighbour. I can almost hear the gossip between Mrs Dean and Mrs Lyon, over the fence between their houses on the opposite side of 8th Street. Mr Lincoln, it seems, was always wandering around strangely dressed, reading books as he went. Why, he often came to the front door in shirt-sleeves and slippers, not the behaviour one expects, dear Mrs Lyon, of a respectable young attorney living in a neighbourhood like ours. And then again, Mrs Dean, the way he spoils those boys! He can never say no to them. They racket around the garden, and in the street, with all those wild pets of theirs – that *mongoose*, Mrs Lyon! – screaming with laughter, getting under everyone's feet – and never once, never *once* have I seen that man rebuke them! No wonder they can never keep a servant more than ten minutes. And what about, Mrs Dean (here the ladies lower their voices rather) – what about all those *rows*?

Rows there certainly were – I can hear them resounding even now. Lincoln was horribly henpecked. Mary hated his loose-limbed untidiness, disregard of convention and lack of domestic enthusiasms, nagging him mercilessly, chiding him for his crude country manners, telling him what he ought to be wearing, sending him on errands. Hour after hour he was obliged to sit in their cramped drawing-room, trying to make small talk as Mary entertained her acquaintances to tea, and explosive indeed was the atmosphere of the house if he ever went to the door in his shirt-sleeves to welcome that nosy Harriet Dean from over the road. He took to spending as much time as possible in his law office, when he often lounged aimlessly about, so we are told, picking up books and putting them down again, looking out of the window or talking to Herndon, now his legal partner. It was noted that when he was out of town on legal business, although it was often perfectly possible for him to get home for the night, he generally preferred to stay at a local inn, swapping yarns half the night with his colleagues: and rather than go to church with Mary on the Sabbath, he would take the boys down to his office, where they behaved deplorably. 'That woman,' as Mrs D. doubtless said to Mrs L., 'why, she makes the man's life a misery!'

But they stayed together. He called her Mother, or sometimes Puss, she called him Mr Lincoln, and the children were a delight to them both, and apparently an embarrassment to neither, even when they came storming in with their menagerie in the middle of a tea party, knocked priceless ornaments to the floor ('Oh dear, that belonged to my great-aunt Harriet, wife of one of President Washington's favourite generals'), or climbed up Lincoln's stretched-out legs and pulled his nose. It was yet another blow to this sad and fated man when Eddie, in his third year, died of cholera in his mother's arms. *Oh why should the spirit of mortal be proud?*

Five minutes' walk took Lincoln from his house to the office he shared with Billy Herndon. The building stood on the corner of the main square, close to the new State House, and it is still there now, largely emblazoned with the words LINCOLN AND HERNDON, and turned into a well-organized museum. By all accounts it was a good deal less orderly when Messrs Lincoln and Herndon occupied the premises. Herndon, despite a merry fondness for alcohol, was tidy and methodical enough, but Lincoln's work systems were sloppy in the extreme. He left documents lying all over the place. He habitually stuffed notes and memoranda in the ribbon of his stove-pipe hat (which looked, Herndon thought, as though a cow had licked it). He lost things, and often lost himself in melancholy and absent-mindedness. Believing, as his English ancestors might have said, that penny wise was pound foolish, he did not much bother himself with matters of petty finance: when the partners shared a fee he simply put Herndon's money in an old box marked 'Billy's Share'. In a big envelope on his desk was written: IF YOU CAN'T FIND IT ANYWHERE ELSE, LOOK IN THIS.

Nevertheless he prospered. He was an efficient and successful attorney in many branches of the law, civil and criminal, and it was as a lawyer, rather than as a politician, that he first stormed the heights of Springfield. Horse thefts and obstructions of the highway, disputes over hog sales or land rights, false insurance claims, attachment suits, physicians' malpractices, matrimonial squabbles, questions of inheritance and transfer, slander, fraud, robbery, murder – all were grist to his mill. He generally gave a human and humorous spin to his conduct of cases – reporting to one client that his case was won, he ended the letter, 'As the Dutch justice said when he married folk, "Now, vere is my hundred tollars?"' – and his reputation put him in touch with citizens of every kind and class. Since as often as not he won his cases, and seems to have been generous in his terms, they made him many friends. So much in demand was he in later years that he pleaded several hundred cases before the Illinois Supreme Court alone.

In the end he became well known as a railroad lawyer – so well known that a brand-new town on the Chicago and Alton Railroad was named Lincoln after him (he christened it personally with juice from a watermelon, and today a stone watermelon slice, mounted on a ped- estal, commemorates the event). As the railways pushed their way across the Middle West in a welter of aspiration, rivalry and sharp practice, they were involved in innumerable legal actions, and Lincoln was frequently consulted, if not embroiled. For example in 1854 he earned his biggest fee ever, $5,000 from the Illinois Central Railroad, by persuading the State Supreme Court that the railway need pay no taxes to counties within the State. Although in fact the Illinois Central thought this fee rather steep, and Lincoln had to sue them to get it, to some of his critics his career could only be tainted by such lucrative associations with big business. Then again, in 1857 he represented the Rock Island Bridge Company, in Illinois, which had built the first railroad bridge across the Mississippi. The company claimed damages when the bridge was hit by a passing steamboat, but the implications of the affair were much wider: the steamboat owners claimed that the bridge was a permanent hazard to river navigation north and south, but Lincoln argued the importance of East–West railroad links over the Mississippi. In this he was not altogether disinterested – he strongly supported the idea of a railroad from New York to San Francisco via Chicago, as against a more southerly route, a plan which would have immense social, economic and political benefits for the Middle West (conspiracy-minded Southerners claim to this day that his private concern with the northern route was a hidden agenda of the civil war).

Still, it is not as a lackey of capitalism that Springfield chiefly remembers Lincoln the lawyer, but as an all-round, run-of-the-mill pleader on the 8th Illinois Judicial Circuit, covering the district north and west of the town. It was a large circuit, at its height including seventeen counties – 120 miles long by 160 miles wide – and the circuit court spent six months of the year travelling around the territory, three in the spring, three in the fall. This peripatetic tribune was a shifting band of old acquaintances, attending their presiding circuit judge like staff around a general. They were nearly all based in Springfield, they all knew each other well, and they travelled together from one small town to another, sometimes only for a few days at a time, sometimes for weeks. There were still few railways in this part of Illinois, the towns were scattered and the roads very rough: as the lawyers laboured here and there, court-house to court-house across the still primitive prairie, they were thrown into one another's company rather as they might be on a military campaign. During his first circuit years Lincoln usually rode his horse Old Buck. Later he acquired a buggy, and one of the most familiar Lincoln images has him lolloping slowly through the countryside, his legs stretched out in front of him, deep in a book while Old Buck patiently navigates the all-too-familiar route. He has an old brown hat on his head and a shawl over his shoulders, and his papers are stuffed into a carpet-bag. Tucked beside him in the buggy is a big green umbrella, missing its knobs, and tied around with string to keep it closed.

It seems a long way around the 8th Judicial Circuit even now, on good tarred roads in a car, but when the weather is right it can be very invigorating. Central Illinois is fine wide farming country, apparently as full of promise now as it was when we first looked at it with the young Lincoln through the trees above the Sangamon River. 'An Effort A Day Keeps Failure Away,' said a popular roadside slogan when I drove around in 1998, doubtless referring to the farming troubles of the time, and for me the area still has an air of down-to-earth, spit-in-the-hand self-reliance. Ranked symmetrically

around their court-house squares, its small country towns
are neat and friendly; the court-houses themselves, sometimes classically domed, sometimes Victorianly Gothic,
are properly self-important. It strikes me as self-
disciplined, welcoming countryside, and its far-scattered
farms, all looking towards the grain elevators and silos of
their nearest town, still form obvious communities. I
stopped my car one day and asked a farmer if he knew
who lived in all the houses that speckled the countryside
as far as I could see, each with its clump of outbuildings.
Without hesitation, sweeping his finger around the horizon, he recited the family names – the Ullendorffs, the
Thomases, the Wolenskis, the Smiths, the Olssens . . .
Some of them are the very same families that were settled
here in Lincoln's time, and in those days, living such
lonely lives away there in the flatlands, when they craved
excitement as often as not they went to the county town
on court day. The arrival of the court, the judge and his
covey of attorneys gave them a change of pace, and they
crowded into the courtroom to listen to the cases.

So except for the unfortunate accused, the progress of
the court was something of a festival, and the company
of lawyers too, seems to have made the most of it.
They were rather like Chaucer's pilgrims on the way to
Canterbury. They had to rough it on the road, because
inns were primitive and accommodations scarce. The
judge might have a room to himself, but the lawyers not
only had to share a room, but even a bed – tough luck
for those obliged to share with the six-foot-four Lincoln,
whose feet invariably protruded from the end of the
blanket, and who often spent much of the night anyway

crouched over a candle with a book. But the evenings downstairs, like the evening at Chaucer's Tabard, were undoubtedly enjoyable, and if Lincoln was not in one of his gloomy moods he could be very good company – right a myrie man, in fact. A lot of shop was doubtless talked, and most of the lawyers drank a good deal, and local people crowded in for the fun of it, and very often Lincoln, draped around his chair in shirt-sleeves and slippers, obliged with some of his tales, or threw in a sample from his book of anecdotes to keep them amused into the small hours. Often the humour was at the expense of his own appearance, and here are a few of the better attested examples of the genre, probably cleaned up over the years, but strung together as I imagine he might have delivered them in a tap-room at Mount Pulaski, or Metamora, or Jacksonville.

'Did you hear that fellow at Tremont call me two-faced? I put it to you, boys, if I had two faces, would I be wearing this one? It puts me in mind of the ugly man who's riding in the woods when he meets an old woman on horseback. "Well, for land's sake," says this ancient crone, "if you're not the homeliest man I ever saw." "Yes, ma'am," says the poor fellow, "I reckon I must be, but I can't help it." "Maybe not," she says, "but at least you might stay at home!" I'll tell you, friends, long ago I took a vow that if I could find a man uglier than myself, I'd shoot him dead there and then. So I took my gun and went out looking for such an unfortunate, and when I found one I told him why I was going to kill him. "You're uglier than I am, and I've taken an oath to murder you." "Well, sir," that man told me, "all I've got to say is this: if I'm really worse-looking than you, for God's sake shoot me, and git me out of the way.'''

In the laughter that greeted this kind of thing, Lincoln's own was sure to be the most infectious, for like my instructor at New Salem he loved his own jokes. He was never a drinker, but he enjoyed the company of drinking men — he once horrified Springfield prohibitionists by declaring publicly that the hearts and heads of habitual drunkards bore 'an advantageous comparison with those of any other class'. No wonder he so often found it more convenient to stop over at the inn, when he could have gone home to Springfield and Mother for the night.

If the ghostly Lincoln really walks through Springfield at midnight he must surely make first, when he leaves his front door, for the corner of Capitol Avenue: for there a striking sight meets the eye. Brilliantly floodlit, five blocks to the east over the railway tracks, there stands the immense and not very beautiful dome of the State Capitol, which Springfield patriots love to tell you is taller than the US Capitol in Washington. This is the city's allegory of allegories, and it greatly stirred me when, wandering about the Lincoln Neighborhood late at night myself, I first saw it standing there like a vision of American Democracy. For all the shenanigans that doubtless go on inside that building — for all the rogues and scoundrels who have been, at one time or another, elected to its membership — for all the corruptions it has witnessed and the conspiracies it has fostered — still it was marvellous to consider, I thought, that out of that very milieu Abe Lincoln had snatched his destiny.

Actually it was not that *physical* milieu, because the present Capitol was not built until the 1880s, but it was certainly that *metaphysical* environment, and Lincoln's ghost would instantly know it still. When the Legislature is not in session Springfield is hardly more than a pleasant country town, but when the two legislative houses convene in their majestic headquarters the whole place comes to life. The Governor presides over caucuses and dinner parties in his solemn mansion, the Capitol swarms with legislators and hangers-on, the hotels fill up with lawyers and journalists, judges abound. The *Journal-Register* finds more exciting matter to report than the annual election of Students of the Year, and even the Poets' and Writers' Forum seems extra effervescent. The car plate SPCHMAKER appears outside the Sangamon Club at lunch-time. A street artist sets up his easel in the main square and exchanges greetings with every passer-by – 'Hi, Mike,' 'Hi Judge' – 'Morning Senator,' 'A very good morning to you, Mike.'

For a stranger it is entertaining then to try guessing who is what in town. 'Are you a member here?' I asked a man in an elevator as we rode to the Senate floor of the Capitol. 'No,' he said, 'but I used to be.' 'You lost an election?' 'That's right, but don't be sorry for me. I was a Senator, now I'm a *lobbyist*!' Lincoln would have understood. Illinois is a big and powerful State now (population 11.5m – more than Greece or Belgium), but even in his time the American democracy was full of puzzles, contradictions, the complications of patronage and the power of the lobby. He would have been perfectly at home among today's inexplicable proceedings in the

Capitol – Bill 168, for instance, proposing stylistic changes in the Mental Health and Development Disabilities Code, or Bill 2887, to amend the School Code relative to reading scores. The rambling drone of the Clerk into his microphone, the leisurely and sociable movements of the members here and there among their swivelling armchairs (well aware of course that they have an audience in the public gallery), the flickering of all their laptop computers, the huddle of reporters interviewing somebody in a corner of the chamber, the habitual buzz of general conversation and the frequent snatches of laughter – all combine to give an impression of collusion and complexity, impenetrable to outsiders, but no doubt clear enough to anyone who had learnt his business with the Long Nine (not to mention the Illinois Central Railroad).

For by the 1850s Lincoln was a well-weathered political careerist. The Whig Party had evolved into the Republican Party, and State Representative Lincoln was a flexible Republican materialist, adept at deals and compromises. His record in Springfield was by no means unspotted. In his day the House met in the smaller and more elegant Old Capitol which they were building when he arrived in town: it is now a museum and a library largely dedicated to his memory, and equipped with recorded birdsong in a sort of homeopathic attempt to keep real starlings off the fabric. In this building Lincoln became as familiar a figure of local politics as he was of the law. His cheerful displays of individualism were well known. Once he leapt out of a window to prevent a quorum. Once he descended into the assembly through a trapdoor in the ceiling. But some of his activities were less frank, and less attractive too. He proved to be adept at manipulation and subterfuge. He wrote scores of anonymous or pseudonymous articles in newspapers, and shamelessly cultivated the Press ('Put it in your pocket, say nothing about it . . .'). He could be so cruel in debate that he once reduced an elderly judge to public tears. His satires were sometimes malicious, sometimes slanderous, and once almost led him into a duel. Even his humour seems to have become more contrived: he complained once, after a speech on a whistle-stop tour, that the train started up 'before the laugh came in'.

Mary Lincoln was privy to much of this, and sometimes colluded in her husband's excesses, but most of it was behind the scenes, and it seldom entered the gossip of the Mrs Deans and Lyons. It is in Lincoln's private letters, and between their lines, that we may sense corrosion setting in. Phrases of disturbing nuance crop up. 'It must not publicly appear that I am paying any attention to the charge,' for example, or 'Don't speak of this, lest they hear of it,' or 'I wish you would let nothing appear in your paper which may operate against me,' or 'The favour I would ask of you is, you will write to Gen. Taylor at once, saying that in your opinion either I, or the man I recommend, shall be appointed to this office.' He wrote hundreds of such letters, setting up meshed ramifications of contact and influence – 'Hi Judge!', as it were. At election times especially he seems to have behaved almost rabidly, and used every category of abuse, mimicry and cunning to advance the Republican cause.

I don't much like the sound of this middle-aged Mr

Lincoln, but there, it was the way of the politician. Besides, as they used to say of children, it was 'only a phase'. Lincoln was too pleased perhaps by his own success, his own cleverness too, and taken over by his own ambition – 'that little organ', as Herndon said, 'that knew no rest'. There was an unpleasant side to his nature, an element of the mountebank, and it seems to me that at Springfield in the 1840s and 1850s he allowed it to predominate. It led him into spite or mayhem, but often enough his kind heart made him sorry.

Lincoln was steeped in the traditions of the Founding Fathers, and he would have been less than human if he had not wished to emulate them. As early as 1838, when he was still new to Springfield, he had told an audience that people of his generation would certainly be seeking new fields of glory. 'Many great and good men,' said he, '. . . may ever be found whose ambition would aspire to nothing beyond a seat in Congress, a gubernatorial or a presidential chair: but such belong not to the family of the lion, or the tribe of the eagle. What! think you these places would satisfy an Alexander, a Caesar, or a Napoleon? Never! Towering genius disdains a beaten path . . . It thirsts and burns for distinction; and if possible it will have it . . .' Ostensibly, of course, Lincoln was warning his audience against the future emergence of tyrants upon the American scene, but there must have been some listeners who recognized then that the young man before them was going to be a politician of almost limitless thrust.

Between 1846 and 1849 Lincoln was a US Congressman in Washington D C, spending the legislative sessions there (sometimes with Mary, sometimes not), returning to Springfield during the recesses. His time in the House of Representatives made little mark, though, and the only stir he caused was when he opposed President Polk's 1846 war against Mexico, which he denounced as morally wrong – Polk, he maintained, had engineered an invasion by making the enemy start a quarrel. It was back in Springfield that he set out to satisfy that thirst for distinction, and what he needed was a grand issue, and a grand platform. Very soon both were available to him.

The great American dispute of the day concerned slavery. The country was divided between the Southern States where it was legal, and the States of the North where it had been outlawed – in seven of them, outlawed since the foundation of the Republic. In the South slavery was generally considered part of the natural order of things, divinely ordained. In the North there was a growing movement for abolition, inflamed by Harriet Beecher Stowe's passionate novel *Uncle Tom's Cabin*, which set out to show, so its author said, 'much of the worst about the institution, and some of the best'. The work had an astonishing effect upon Northern public opinion, selling in its hundreds of thousands of copies. I read it for the first time in the course of writing this book, in a tattered mid-Victorian family copy my great-grandfather, I suppose, bought in far-away Britain. It has a preface by the Right Honourable the Earl of Carlisle, who says it marked 'a kind of epoch in the moral history of the time'. A century and a half later I was powerfully affected by it still, although the very name of Uncle Tom, its saintly black hero, had by then acquired altogether different connotations.

They called American slavery the Peculiar Institution, and it was certainly a paradox in a country so dedicated to ideas of liberty and modernity – almost everywhere else in the Western world the very idea of it was anachronistic anathema. A measure called the Missouri Compromise, dating from the 1820s, maintained the status quo, drawing a border between the two systems which became known as the Mason-Dixon line. The situation was ambiguous, though. The Compromise forbade the extension of slavery into any parts of the country not already settled; yet the Fugitive Slave Law of 1793 still allowed runaway slaves to be arrested anywhere in the Republic, and returned to their owners. The foreign slave-trade had long been banned; but the buying and selling of human beings was perfectly legal in Virginia, the Carolinas, Maryland, Delaware, Missouri, Tennessee, Kentucky, Texas and Florida – and within the District of Columbia, the Vatican of American freedom. By the 1850s tempers on the issue, on both sides of the Mason-Dixon line, ran perilously high. Abolitionists in the North provocatively abetted the Underground Railway, a system of clandestine escape routes by which slaves were whisked away to freedom in British Canada – 'the blessed shores of England', as Mrs Stowe called it. Zealots in the South swore that no human agency would make them abandon the very basis of their heritage, their culture, their economy and their famous chivalry. There was talk already of the Union breaking up.

Lincoln was familiar enough with slavery. Kentucky

was a slave State, and Little Pigeon Creek, his second childhood home, stood beside a public road: he was certainly quite used to seeing manacled black people travelling by. His father was alleged to have been in dispute with some of the local chapel worthies because of his abolitionist views: at least in later life Lincoln thought it expedient to tell it so, but it may just have been that Tom Lincoln thought slave labour unfair competition to his own kind – a familiar syndrome in the poor white country. The boy Lincoln probably did not think twice about the Peculiar Institution, and was no more shocked by the sight of black humans in chains than a contemporary English colonial child would have been shocked by scenes of Indian poverty. His sensibilities may perhaps have been affronted, as myth said, by what he saw during his river-voyages into the deep South, but he seems to have expressed no particular thoughts about slavery until he was well into his forties.

By then his views on race in general were probably no more liberal, and no less, than those of most decent Americans of the day. He wished the Negroes no harm, but did not consider them his equals, intellectually or morally. He certainly did not believe in universal suffrage for black people. Ideally he would have liked the two races to live separately – segregated, in fact – preferably by the repatriation of American Negroes to the lands they had come from, or their settlement in new colonies of their own outside the United States. In the mean time, the least one could do for the black man was leave him alone.

His attitude to slavery itself was more ambivalent, and

his personal circumstances helped to make it so. He had married, after all, into a slave-owning family. Back in Kentucky the Todds were deeply entrenched in the system, and when Lincoln paid a visit to them with Mary he found himself in the middle of it too. The Todd house on West Main Street in Lexington is a pleasant if rather cramped early-nineteenth-century house, now a national monument. In the 1840s it was cluttered with Victorian knick-knacks and conversation pieces, and stiff with good manners – hardly an easy ambience for the long-limbed and unconventional Lincoln. And as for the hired help *chez* Todd – well, it was not hired at all. It was owned. Around the house a clutter of shacks and outbuildings contained half-a-dozen human beings who were as absolutely the Todds' private property as the drawing-room sofas. When a meal was served it was brought by a slave from the kitchen at the end of the garden. When a mint julep was needed a slave mixed it – nobody could mix a better julep than the Todd's old Nelson. When Lincoln was taken to visit the family cotton-mill he found it was worked by slave labour under the assistant managership of his own brother-in-law.

Just down the road from the Todds' house, in Court House Square, men, women and children were regularly auctioned precisely like domestic animals, and if Lincoln looked out of the right window, he could see the slave pens of Lewis C. Roberts, Negro Buyer. If he picked up the local paper, he was sure to find announcements of slave sales: I tried it myself one day by opening almost at random an issue of the *Lexington Gazette* from the 1840s, and at once came across an advertisement offering the Entire Contents of a Farm, including Valuable Harness Horses, a fine stock of Grazier Hogs and Twenty Likely Negroes (plus several Children). Slavery was part of the very atmosphere of Lexington, part of the air the Todd family had breathed from childhood, and if Lincoln was embarrassed by the tea-party gentility on West Main Street, how did he feel when a living black chattel entered the parlour with fresh sandwiches on a silver tray?

And yet . . . if the idea of slavery was hideous, at its best the slave-based culture of the South was undeniably attractive, not least to a sensitive man like Lincoln with an uncertain place in society. About 60 miles west of Lexington is the more appealing city of Louisville, on the Ohio River, and here Abe had a different experience of the institution. This was more like the Old South of wistful legend, the chivalric magnolia-and-crinoline South. After his rejection by Mary in 1841 Lincoln went there by steamboat from Illinois to recuperate in the hospitality of his friend Joshua Speed, a Springfield merchant of a well-known Louisville family (and some suggest his lover). I like to think of him disembarking from his stern-wheeler down at the levee, where the oldest working steamship on the river, *The Belle of Louisville*, still lies ornately at the wharf, and the great river is crossed now by four steel bridges in parallel. I watched out for him one day from the deck of the Little Annie Towboat Café, moored near by, and fancied him in his tall hat and fustian coat treading stork-like down the *Belle*'s gangplank, to be whisked away in a spanking buggy to Farmington, the Speed home on the outskirts of town. Down a long, narrow, leafy lane the fine high-trotting horse takes him, and across well-tended lawns, to deposit him at the door of one of the most delightful country houses imaginable.

Farmington was built to Palladian plans drawn up by Thomas Jefferson himself and is a small archetype of pre-bellum Southern elegance, in the Virginia manner. It is a show house now and has long been overtaken by Louisville's urban sprawl, but it is still wonderfully inviting – not at all pretentious, symmetrical in an easy classical way and surrounded still by lawns, gardens and a lovely wide orchard. Here Abraham steps out of his carriage, Morocco the black coachman stands by the door with his hat in his hand, and here is Josh Speed crying, 'Lincoln, my dear fellow, come in, come in and meet the family': and instantly – who can doubt it? – melancholy Abe is entranced. It is like Waugh's *Brideshead*: the clever, imaginative, impressionable young man out of a lower social stratum bewitched by an upper-class style, and perhaps discerning it as properly his own.

Here it was the style of slavery. Lincoln spent three weeks at Farmington, and I bet he loved it. The house was cool and elegant – much the best house he had ever stayed in. Speed's family was delightful. A personal slave looked after him. He walked with his friend through the orchard and over the wide meadows behind, and read his books on a bench in the shade. He revelled, I am sure, in the serene good taste of the estate and the respectful courtesy of its slaves, but he must have seen that the beauty of Farmington consorted awkwardly with the evil of it. 'Massa Lincoln, sir, your bath is ready,' I hear a comfortable voice crying from the porch of the house; and Lincoln puts away his book, stifles his scruples and strolls back through the herb garden to the creature comforts of injustice.

If it troubled his personal conscience, the Peculiar Institution tangled his political attitudes, too. He thought it was wicked, but he did not think it should be abolished, because the United States Constitution apparently allowed the several States to do what they wished about it – slavery was never mentioned by name in that hallowed code, but slaves presumably came under the category of property, and property was sacrosanct. He believed it was an outmoded economic system anyway, and was bound to fade away before long in an advanced modern society, but he was a man of the law, and did not hesitate, in 1847, to accept as a client a Kentucky slave-holder who wanted a slave of his forcibly returned from Illinois. In Lincoln's mind the awkward ambiguity of it all came to a head when in 1854 the US Senate passed a measure called the Kansas–Nebraska Act, which overruled the Missouri Compromise and allowed the extension of slavery, if a majority of the people wanted it, into newly settled districts of the West.

Here was his issue! Lincoln declared himself astounded, thunderstruck and stunned, and stormed into political battle. As always, though, he stormed carefully. Within his own party there were differences on the future of slavery. Radicals demanded its immediate abolition; moderates wanted it held in check or allowed to dissolve by historical and economic evolution; right-wingers were all for it – not least in the southern parts of Lincoln's

own State, Illinois. He had to be tactful, then. To one
audience he would emphasize his abhorrence of the
institution, to another he would stress his devotion
to the Constitution. Here he talked about the natural
rights of the Negro race, there he made it clear that
there never could be equality between the black and
white peoples. The further south he talked in Illinois,
it was said of him, the whiter his principles were. He
brought to these fateful matters some of the sleight of
hand he had learnt during his years in local politics, but
he knew now that his destiny was to be grander, and
that these immense national controversies were more to
his proper scale. He widened his invective, from the
personal to the almost abstract, and he talked a lot about
a sinister combination popularly known as the Slave
Power.

This was not just another conspiracy theory. The
slave-owning interests of the South, and their allies in
the North, really were formidably powerful in the affairs
of the Union. Rumour said the Legislature, the US
Supreme Court and the Presidency itself had all been
subverted by the Slave Power; and when in 1857 the
US Supreme Court ruled that Negroes could not be
United States citizens, and that Congress could not lawfully exclude slavery from newly settled territories, it
really was the result of improper collusion between the
Democratic President Buchanan and the Chief Justice.
The next step in the conspiracy, Lincoln maintained,
would be a further Supreme Court decision declaring
that no State of the Union could lawfully exclude slavery,
and eventually the whole country would be a Slave

Power – perhaps a Slave Empire, extending its system throughout Latin America, where various Southern fili-busters were already setting up little dominions of their own.

On the other hand, the Northern abolitionists were becoming ever more militant – much too militant for Lincoln – and they found a fanatic champion in John Brown, a Connecticut farmer of Pilgrim descent. Brown was a half-crazed detester of slavery who reminds me of contemporary imperialists of the British Empire, raging through the Punjab armoured in self-righteousness and fired by Biblical example. Brown roved the nation like a man possessed, preaching the abolitionist cause and threatening violence upon all slave-owners. 'Without shedding of blood there is no remission of sin,' he liked to cry, and he had heady plans for a free republic of ex-slaves. Convinced the blacks of the South could easily be encouraged into rebellion against their masters, he led a gang of activists in a mad attack upon a Federal arsenal at Harper's Ferry, on the Virginia side of the Potomac River. He was easily trapped and presently executed, but his furious soul marched on to the rhythm of 'John Brown's Body Lies A-Mouldering in the Grave' . . . soon to be metamorphosed into the great Battle Hymn of the Republic.

This was not at all Lincoln's style. Between 1854 and 1860 Lincoln made 175 speeches concerning slavery, and in all of them he stuck to his principle that it could not be constitutionally abolished. At the same time he proclaimed his belief that the Declaration of Independ-ence had meant just what it said when it decreed that all men were created equal. The Declaration was the original basis for the existence of the Republic, and unlike the Constitution it could not be amended. Did he really think that when the slave-owner Thomas Jefferson wrote its resounding words, he was thinking of black people as well as white? I doubt it. Few in the eighteenth century, and not many more in the nine-teenth, believed that the Negro race was as entirely human as the Caucasian. Perhaps it was even true, as proponents of the Slave Power claimed, that the Declar-ation was not even referring to white people in general: it was really no more than a rebellious tract, and was merely claiming that everyone born under the British Crown was politically equal whether they lived in Britain or in the colonies. Lincoln himself believed the physical differences between blacks and whites would 'for ever forbid the two races living together on terms of political and social equality': as much as any other man, he said, he was in favour of having 'the superior position assigned to the white race'. But if the Republic was to survive, it had eventually to decide on slavery one way or the other. 'A house divided against itself cannot stand,' he cried in his first nationally influential speech, delivered in the State House at Springfield. 'I believe this government cannot endure, permanently half-slave and half-free.'

The chief begetter of the Kansas–Nebraska Act was Lincoln's great Democratic rival in Illinois politics (and perhaps in love): the smooth and accomplished Stephen Douglas, nicknamed the Little Giant because he was five foot four inches tall but a mighty orator – a mighty drinker too, and a man of great charm. It was this combination, of a tremendous issue and a charismatic opponent, that finally projected Lincoln towards his field of glory.

Let us visit, one day in 1858, the village of Havana in Illinois. It is a small port on the Illinois River, not far upstream from Beardstown, and its most interesting feature is a circular Indian mound overlooking the river. This is thought to date from the second century A D, and was once the site of tribal courts and meetings.

This afternoon it is the scene of a political meeting in support of Stephen Douglas, Democratic candidate for an Illinois seat in the US Senate. He has arrived with a flourish on his private train, announcing himself with a blast from the cannon mounted on one of its wagons, and a large festive crowd has streamed out from the town to hear him speak, with flags and streamers and rosettes, clambering up the slopes of the grassy mound and pressing upon the dignitaries seated in their ranked chairs on its summit. Douglas welcomes them suavely, a neat and formidable little figure. He is one of the best-known orators in America, and he speaks as the worldly politician he is, expressing himself clearly, competently, with elegance, but with just enough vitriol to show he is not a silver-voiced charmer.

Still, he does talk for two hours, and perhaps attention is just starting to waver when there is the chug of a paddle-wheel from the river, the loud blast of a steam-whistle and the blare of a band. The steamboat *Editor* is arriving from Beardstown, and down its gangplank stalks for all to see Douglas's Republican opponent in the con-test, Mr Abraham Lincoln of Springfield. Half the crowd scatters down the slope to meet him. The whistle blows again, the band plays lustily on the *Editor*'s deck, and here comes longshank Lincoln striding like Quixote up the Indian mound, surrounded by welcoming Republicans, to be greeted with a handshake from the very sophisticated Sancho at the top. Such was the style of the Lincoln-Douglas debates of 1858, which were to enter American history, and alter Lincoln's life for good.

The disputants really were rather like fictional figures, the long and the short of it, six foot four v. five foot four, but actually they were wonderfully well matched. They campaigned mercilessly but generally courteously. Besides the usual contests of the husting, as at Havana, it was arranged that they should meet each other in formal confrontations, to be held at different Illinois locations over a three-month period. Throughout the State markers still identify the sites. The sole subject of debate was slavery, which now obsessed the whole nation, and the lines were quite clearly drawn. Douglas was for the continuance of slavery, and even its extension; Lincoln was against, but wanted the institution to be allowed to die a natural death. The rivals' manners were distinct, too – Douglas suave but showy, Lincoln exploiting the power of his home-bred idiomatic rhetoric: by now he had become such a master of popular audiences that 'every one of his stories,' Douglas said, 'seems like a whack upon my back.' Douglas tried to exhibit Lincoln as a dangerous radical on questions of race and slavery; Lincoln was out to show that Douglas wanted to make slavery not merely permanent, but also legal throughout the Republic. Usually they spoke alternately – Lincoln/Douglas/Lincoln at one town, Douglas/Lincoln/Douglas at the next – and generally on the court-house floor to serious and deeply committed audiences, who often intervened with questions and comments, groans or laughter.

The debates made Lincoln nationally famous. So burning an issue was slavery then, so remarkable were the two debaters, that their contests were reported at length all over the country – more widely reported than many a Presidential election. The texts of the Lincoln-Douglas debates were to be reprinted for ever after, and the name of Abraham Lincoln became known in every literate home. Douglas it was who went to the Senate, but then he was famous anyway. Lincoln was the real winner. Soon he was greeted as a celebrity everywhere. In New York he gave a speech at the Cooper Institute in which he demonstrated, in a lawyerly way, that in the matter of slavery he and the Republican party were merely sticking to the 'old and tried policy' of the Founding Fathers – to accept the status quo, while branding slavery as a moral evil. 'As these fathers marked it, so let it be again marked, as an evil not to be extended, but to be tolerated and protected only because of and as far as its actual presence among us makes that toleration and protection a necessity.'

And so long as it was expedient, that remained his opaque manifesto, whether as a provincial politician or as President of the United States.

President of the United States! Mary Todd had always foreseen it; Abraham Lincoln had undoubtedly dreamed

of it; in his last years at Springfield the stir caused by
the Lincoln-Douglas debates made it a political likeli-
hood. Lincoln had become unquestionably the leading
Republican in Illinois, a figure to be reckoned with by
Republicans everywhere, and he had engaged himself
very publicly in the overwhelming issue of the day. He
was at odds with the militantly radical wing of the party,
which demanded the complete abolition of slavery in
the United States, but he had managed to keep in balance
most of the other factions. We see him now, his ambition
hardened, as a supremely subtle and manipulative politician, all too well aware how absolutely the American
democracy depended upon quid pro quo and compromise. On the one hand he was the experienced attorney,
dedicated, so he said, to the law of reason, on the other the
populist one-of-a-kind, always ready to break tension, or
clinch an argument, with a homespun aphorism or a
joke. Ordinary people loved 'Old Abe', 'Honest Abe',
so informal and unconventional. They seldom realized
how calculated were his techniques, but they certainly
now saw him as a potential President.

Mary kept him at it, and before long a web of friends,
supporters and cronies of varied motive were pressing for
his adoption as Republican candidate in the Presidential
election of 1860. First the State party had to choose its
own nominee at a convention in Decatur, where Lincoln
had made his first political speech, barefoot on the stump,
so many years before. This was to be crucial to his
reputation ever after, because half-way through the proceedings there burst into the hall one of the awful Hanks
clan, the indigent familiars of his youth. John Hanks

carried one of those half-logs we saw used at a fence at New Salem, together with a banner announcing that it had been split by Abe Lincoln himself, that simple son of the people. So Lincoln acquired his most familiar epithet, the Railsplitter, and so he won the nomination of the Illinois Republicans.

The next stage was the Republican national convention in Chicago, which would finally adopt the party's candidate to fight the election for the Presidency. Lincoln's only serious opponent was William Seward, a gentlemanly New Yorker. A large wooden building, nicknamed the Wigwam, was especially built for the occasion on Lake Street, at the edge of today's Loop. It could hold at least ten thousand people. Chicago itself was then in a condition of violent and convulsive growth, a terrible but mighty mess of a place. The convention was rather the same. Thousands of party supporters flooded into the town, wheeling and dealing, conspiring, plotting coups and counter-coups: supporters of Seward relatively restrained, supporters of Lincoln, all but a native son, altogether more vulgar. We see them in old magazine engravings packed in their thousands in the great ramshackle structure, cliques jammed against cliques, huddles of fixers around the doors, reporters scribbling everywhere, bands often playing, processions coming and going all day long.

Lincoln was not there in person – he stayed at home in Springfield – but some unscrupulous work was done on his behalf. Dubious promises were made in his name. Deals were arranged that would return to plague him. Railroads were persuaded to give free tickets to his supporters. Galleries were packed with noisy shouters, to keep Seward's people out, and when Lincoln's name was called, so one reporter wrote, a roar went up 'like all the hogs ever slaughtered in Cincinnati giving their death squeals together . . .' It worked. The Railsplitter won. After a third ballot, the convention unanimously endorsed him as the Republican candidate for the Presidency. The Democrats were helplessly divided among themselves, and three months later Abraham Lincoln was elected sixteenth President of the United States – the very first Republican President.

At the end of 1860 the Union was on the verge of disintegration, facing a war between the States: Lincoln had found a challenge worthy of the Founding Fathers themselves, not to mention the tribe of lions and eagles.

'Can it be possible?' an English resident of Springfield is supposed to have expostulated. 'Abe Lincoln! – a man that buys a ten-cent beefsteak for his breakfast, and carries it home himself!' But almost at once thousands of letters arrived at Springfield, thousands of visitors too, to offer the President-elect congratulations, petitions, proposals, complaints and recriminations. An eleven-year-old girl from Westfield, New York, wrote suggesting a beard would improve his appearance ('You would look a great deal better for your face is so thin'): Lord Charnwood was to characterize her as 'a dreadful young person', but Lincoln took her advice and started to grow one, transforming himself once and for all into the Lincoln of all our images.

Now he was the hero of Springfield indeed, and

before he left for Washington a Republican procession of honour paraded past the house at 8th and Jackson. What a glory that was! Springfield took to the streets that day, and the parade took eight hours to pass the Lincoln house. Mrs Dean, Mrs Lyon and all the neighbours hung from their windows, and as the floats and wagons and marching men went by, swarms of well-wishers crowded into the house to shake Mr Lincoln's hand, pat Tad and Willie kindly on the head and offer their respectful regards to Mrs Lincoln. We can see the scene now in a photograph taken from across the street. On the road itself the procession trundles slowly by – notably, at our particular moment, a wagon covered with muslin and foliage containing thirty-three celebratory maidens, all in white, representing the States of the Union. The pavements are jammed with male onlookers, shirtsleeved because of the summer sun but one and all hatted – in top hats, in fedoras, in sailor caps, in straw hats. Behind them the Lincoln house is besieged by well-wishers, crowded tight on the terrace and the sidewalk, waving their hats exultantly. There is Mrs Lincoln, stately in a bonnet at a downstairs window, and upstairs Willie looks out, pale from a recent bout with the scarlet fever ('Can you wonder?' say Mrs D. and Mrs L. 'Poor little mite').

And standing beside his own front door, head and shoulders above the rest, uncharacteristically smart in a white suit and a bow tie, stands Mr Lincoln. He looks rather pale himself. '*That's* no surprise,' says Mrs D. 'The unfortunate man spent half the day yesterday writing his own labels on his luggage. I saw him with my own eyes over the back fence, not that I'm one to pry. "A. Lincoln, The White House," he was sitting there on the porch writing it over and over again, as if he were some kind of flunkey. I suppose that woman made him do it.'

'Well,' says Mrs L., 'she's got what she wanted now.'

Transition: All Aboard!

On the wet morning of 11 February 1861, Lincoln went with Mary to the Great Western railway station at Springfield to board the train for Washington and the White House. A crowd of well-wishers went with him, clamouring to shake his hand, and while the locomotive hissed and the rain drooped down, he stood on the rear platform of his coach and made a farewell speech – scribbled on the back of an envelope, according to legend. This is what he said:

My friends

No one, not in my situation, can appreciate my feeling of sadness at this parting. To this place, and the kindness of these people, I owe everything. Here I have lived a quarter of a century, and have passed from a young to an old man. Here my children have been born, and one is buried. I now leave, not knowing when, or whether ever, I may return, with a task before me greater than that which rested upon Washington.

Without the assistance of that Divine Being, who ever attended him, I cannot succeed. With that assistance I cannot fail. Trusting in Him, who can go with me, and remain with you and be everywhere for good, let us confidently hope that all will yet be well. To His care commending you, as I hope in your prayers you will commend me, I bid you an affectionate farewell.

The whistle blew, the conductor cried 'All aboard!', the train lurched and was on its way.

Four

*President of misery — an unlovely maelstrom — groping — war begins —
Lincoln's Washington — lackadaisical genius? — the only man — a politician
still — something transcendental — family troubles — race, slavery and emancipation — 'a kind of poetry' — ready for death*

Abraham Lincoln, sixteenth President of the United
States of America, was a president of misery. He was the
only incumbent in history whose term of office was
completed entirely in wartime, and the sixteenth Presidency was the saddest there ever was. His Republic was
hideously divided, and under his authority at least 360,000
of his people died in battle. For much of the time the
armies of which he was the Commander-in-Chief
suffered humiliating defeats. He lost a second son, his
wife sank into mental illness, from first to last he was
beset by political enemies within and without his own

party. His capital was a hotbed of conspiracy and disloyalty, and in the end he was murdered there.

He entered Washington, as it happened, in a skuldug
way himself. His train journey from Springfield had
been a triumphal progress, with civic celebrations and
opportunities for publicity all the way: at Westfield, New
York, he even went out of his way to kiss Grace Bedell,
the 'dreadful young person' who was responsible for his
new beard — 1861's equivalent of a soundbite. In the
course of the protracted journey, however, word reached
his security people that an attempt was to be made on
his life at Baltimore, capital of the slave State of Maryland.
He was switched to another and less ostentatious train,
and sneaked into Washington incognito, preposterously
disguised, according to derisory cartoonists, in a Scotsman's tartan kilt, cloak and tam-o'-shanter. Instead of
going straight to the White House he was rushed in a
curtained coach to Willard's Hotel, a cauldron of political
exchange and intrigue, and so was introduced to the
atmosphere of suspicion, conspiracy and latent threat that
was to be endemic to the Washington of his Presidency.

Still endemic, for that matter. When I myself arrived
in the capital to start work on this book, Washington
was in the midst of one of its perennial political scandals,
abuzz with controversy and innuendo. The very moment
I crossed the Arlington Memorial Bridge into the city
centre, a screaming motorcade hurled all other traffic off
the highway and rushed past me in a flurry of motorcycle
police, black stretch limousines and cars full of black-
suited secret agents peering over each other's shoulders.
I have no idea who was the figure at the heart of this

sinister display, but it occurred to me that when Lincoln was smuggled into town in 1861 it must have all felt rather the same. The country was about to plunge into civil war then – the greatest of all national scandals. The city was alive with rumour and subterfuge. Reporters were everywhere, and Lincoln entered into his glory heavily guarded. To this day people of all kinds turn up at Willard's in vehicles with smoked or curtained windows. 'Sure thing,' I was told by a doorman one evening when I was hanging around the sidewalks there, 'we have limos coming here night and day, and you never know who's goin' to be in 'em. I've seen 'em all – Nixon, Reagan, Bush, Ford, Clinton, you name them.' 'Lincoln?' 'Mr Lincoln? Sure, why not.'

Washington DC was a small city of the American South, designed specifically as a capital. Today it sprawls far beyond the diamond enclave of the District of Columbia, far beyond even the terrifying Beltway which surrounds the city like a howling rampart, far into Virginia in the South, Maryland and Delaware to the East. In Lincoln's day it was a compact place of some 61,000 people, 11,000 of them black, in an incipient condition. Much of it was unfinished. The US Capitol, which had been burnt by the British during the war of 1812, was still without its dome. The Washington Memorial obelisk was incomplete, and work on it was temporarily abandoned due to lack of funds and interest. Pigs, goats and cows wandered the streets. All around the Government centre horrible stinks arose from the Chesapeake Canal, which passed sluggishly less than a mile from the Executive Mansion

– the White House, as it was already called, although it was far from white. Drinking water was drawn from the horribly polluted Potomac River; typhoid, malaria, dysentery and tuberculosis were all endemic. No wonder staff at the British Embassy, then and for another century, qualified for hazard pay.

To make things far worse, when Lincoln arrived from Springfield in March 1861 the whole place had been thrown into turmoil by the imminent probability of civil war. Troops were encamped all over the place. Work was starting on a ring of sixty-eight defensive forts around the perimeter of the city. Arsenals, hospitals, cannon parks, barracks, remount depots, commissary warehouses – all were springing up in a muddied frenzy of activity, and the rutted streets were a perpetual commotion of wagons and weaponry and marching men. There was a military slaughterhouse on the Mall, and a rabble of hustlers, traders, thieves and con men had followed the flag into town, giving it an air of raffish squalor. A new quarter of gambling houses and brothels appeared close to the Government centre (Mme Russell's Bake Oven, Gentle Annie Lyle's Place), and was later nicknamed General Hooker's Division after a commander whose name was consequently to enter the language (so it is claimed by his admirers) as a feminine noun.

Washington was surrounded on all sides by slave-owning States. In 1861 its social élite was still almost entirely Southern, snobbish, stylish and confident – Southerners had dominated the Presidency and the Congress almost since the birth of the Republic. There were slave pens within sight of Willard's, for slavery was legal in the District of Columbia – Lincoln once called the whole place 'a sort of Negro livery stable'. On 3rd Street and Constitution Avenue the St Charles Hotel, the equivalent of a good county hotel in England or Australia, advertised 'roomy underground cells for confining slaves for safe keeping', and assured patrons that if their slaves escaped, 'full value of the Negro will be paid by the Proprietor'. Virginia, the Old Dominion, the grandest part of the South, was just over the Potomac River, and the beautiful plantations along the James River, the epitome of Southern loftiness and tradition, the loveliest expressions of the slave culture, were less than 50 miles away.

The White House itself, into which the President and his family presently moved, stood in its own garden in the heart of all this squalor. It was a run-down mansion whose theme tune was very properly the cheap and brassy anthem 'Hail to the Chief'. One observer likened it to an unsuccessful hotel, and Lincoln himself dismissed it as 'this damned old house'. Poor Abe, fifty-two years old and now transformed by the black mutton-chop beard which was to be his distinguishing feature for the rest of his life – poor fellow, to come from dear old Springfield, where nearly everyone was a friend, into this noisy, unwelcoming, untrustworthy and unlovely maelstrom of power! Of course he knew what to expect: he had lived in Washington before, and he was used to the loveless entanglements of politics. He must have been homesick all the same, for that pleasant house on 8th and Jackson. 'If there's a worse place than hell,' he wrote in a moment of despair, 'I'm in it.'

★

In effect the civil war began on Lincoln's very first day in office. It had been rumbling for months, around the inescapable issue of slavery, and had come to a head specifically because of his election to the Presidency. He was a known enemy to the idea of human bondage. He had carried all the free States, none of the slave States, and Southerners were convinced that he would bring about the end of the Peculiar Institution, and with it the end of their lifestyle and prosperity. While the States of the North had embraced every modernity, already making themselves into an industrial force of unrivalled potential, the States of the South had stuck to their antique agricultural system, and the plantation society based upon it. It was a tribal kind of society, like the Scotland of the clans, and it depended upon slavery. Landowners relied upon forced black labour because it was ideal for the production of rice and cotton in their hot climate. Poor whites supported it because it gave them social status: a white was a white was a white, whether he were millionaire or pauper. But in a more potent way, white Southerners were convinced that upon slavery depended their whole cherished mystique, their whole tradition of leisured and elegant living, their love of the soil, their chivalric notions of themselves, their myths of lacy romance.

When I first went to the American South myself, ninety-odd years later, I found myself as a foreigner sucked into this climate of resentful illusion. No Northerner could ever understand, I was told, the links of loyalty and family unity that had bound the Southern gentry to their slaves, and made of their society something uniquely civilized in the world. For that matter no European could be expected to understand the indestructible God-ordained differences that must for ever keep the black man in subjection to the white. 'Class counts, you know – I loved my old black nanny dearly – they want segregation themselves, just as much as we do – there's a morality in self-preservation – how would you feel if your daughter married a nigrah?' These were incantations coming to me directly from Lincoln's own America. They were streaked with malice, and even in the 1950s, when I ventured to resist them in private conversation, I found myself publicly pilloried in an editorial in the Charleston *News and Courier* . . .

When Lincoln was elected it was the last straw. To many citizens of the slave States secession seemed the only riposte. 'Let the consequences be what they may,' said one Georgia newspaper, 'whether the Potomac is crimsoned in human gore, and Pennsylvania Avenue is paved ten fathoms deep with mangled bodies . . . the South will never submit to such humiliation and degradation as the inauguration of Abraham Lincoln.' Faced as they thought with the forced abolition of slavery throughout the United States, one by one the eleven States south of the Mason-Dixon line broke away from the Union to form a sovereign Confederacy of their own: its president was Jefferson Davis, Kentucky grandson of an immigrant from Wales. South Carolina was the first to go and when Lincoln actually became President the *grand seigneur* of them all, Virginia, disowned his authority too.

Lincoln groped a way through these developments.

He had long before declared it the right of any people, if enough of them agreed, to overthrow their existing form of Government by revolution. What American patriot could argue otherwise? Now he said the 'central idea' of the Union argument against secession was 'the necessity of proving that popular government is not an absurdity . . . We must settle this question now, whether in a free government the minority have the right to break up the government when they choose.' But a huge enfranchised majority in the South was merely demanding autonomy for its own territory – itself considerably larger than Europe – and there was nothing in the US Constitution to deny it that right. Such problems, for a Presidential lawyer! And behind all the President's thinking was his own ambivalent approach to the matter of slavery itself, the cause of all these troubles and the great quandary of America – legal but immoral, seductive but abhorrent. 'Let the only shout of triumph over its final adjustment,' wrote the distant Earl of Carlisle in his preface to *Uncle Tom's Cabin*, 'be the Hallelujahs of the Heavens.' Easy to say, President Lincoln might have replied.

The climactic showdown came in April. By then the Union and the Confederacy had become *de facto* enemies, if not actually at war, certainly not at peace with each other. Many of the formerly Federal military installations in the South had already been taken over by Confederate forces, but one of the most symbolically important remained in Union hands. This was the island fortress of Sumter, which commanded the harbour of Charleston in South Carolina – the first State to secede and perhaps the most fervently pro-slavery. Fort Sumter dominated (as it still does) the sea approach to Charleston, humped there in the water like a squat gatekeeper to the lovely towered and pillared city, and the Stars and Stripes that flew above it was a bitter provocation to the Charlestonians. The Confederates had not tried to seize the fort, but they were refusing to allow provisions to reach its small garrison, and Lincoln had hardly reached his Presidential desk when he was faced with a fearful decision: whether to sustain Sumter by force, whether to launch pre-emptive strikes on Charleston city, or whether to surrender the fort to the Southerners. Did he remember President Polk, goading the Mexicans into firing the first shot? He decided to send a ship-load of food and ammunition to the fort; and so it was that on 12 April 1861 rebel artillery from the South Carolina mainland fired the original salvos of the American civil war and very soon forced Sumter's surrender.

Lincoln ordered the mobilization of 70,000 militia and declared a blockade of Southern ports, and the war formally began. Few wars have been so muddled. The enemies were not natural enemies, but were often friends and relatives. All the lines were blurred. In every Southern State there were loyal Unionists, and many Northerners sympathized with the South. Four of the slave States did not secede, but were racked with violent and dissenting views: the western part of Virginia split from the rest of the State, set itself up as the State of Kanawha and presently joined the Union as West Virginia. Anomalies abounded – for instance Chincoteague, a Virginian island off the ocean shore, found the ties of trade with the

North more profitable than any ties of loyalty to the
South, and stuck with the Union throughout the war.
Lincoln himself was so shaken by the desertion of one
of his most trusted officers to the Confederacy that his
confidence was shaken in everybody, he said, and he
hardly knew who to trust any more.

It was an intimate sort of conflict. Jefferson Davis,
having first established the headquarters of the Confederacy at Montgomery in Alabama, presently removed it to
Richmond, Virginia, only 80 miles from Washington
itself: and so the hostile capitals stood (so Winston
Churchill fancied) 'like queens at chess upon adjacent
squares'.

I assume it was with a sense of European superiority that
my great-grandfather, Harriet Beecher Stowe in hand,
looked across the Atlantic to the iniquities of American
slavery: and I, too, cannot help observing the Washington
of the sixteenth Presidency slightly *de haut en bas*. To
anyone brought up, however vicariously, to the
nineteenth-century dignities of Buckingham Palace, the
Vatican or the Elysée Palace, Lincoln's White House
does seem to have offered a most dishevelled contrast.
Gradually its dinginess and dilapidation disappeared
under the management of Mary, who spent sums excru-
ciatingly beyond her official budget in doing the old
place up, equipping it with fancy curtains and furniture
and imposing her own pretentious taste upon it all. Even
so, it remained a kind of public gallery. Anyone could
wander in, it seems, when the doors opened at 9 a.m.
each day, to take a look at things, to take a look at the

President, and pester him with requests for jobs and favours. He was the People's Abraham after all, and he believed in the right of access. He spent endless hours talking to people of all sorts, exchanging ideas with politicians, businessmen, soldiers, religious leaders, place-seekers by the hundred, calming angry complainants and humouring a multitude of cranks. Sometimes he felt that each visitor took away a little of his own vitality 'with thumb and finger', leaving him at the end of the day in a condition of – his own word – flabbiness. There were guards about of course, and Lincoln was protected too by three devoted aides: his hefty bodyguard Thomas Lamon, an old Springfield friend, and two young secre-taries, John G. Nicolai and John Hay, who thought he was the greatest character since Christ. Nevertheless the pressure upon Lincoln was so unremitting, from morning until night, that he sometimes thought (so he told a friend) the only escape would be to run away and hang himself from a tree on the lawn outside.

Was there ever a stranger setting for the Chief Execu-tive of a great Power? What would Bismarck have thought, or Disraeli, or Pius IX? Crowds of people bustled here and there, up and down stairs, wearing top hats, check trousers, voluminous skirts, mourning bonnets – peering into doors, inspecting the décor, clutching letters of introduction or proposal, arguing with sentries, pleading with secretaries, lining up outside the President's own office in the hope of a word or even a glimpse. The house was not merely the President's office, either. It was his home too, and haughtily through the hubbub we may imagine Mrs Lincoln advancing to

order an embellishment here, a removal there. Robert
had been away to boarding school and Harvard, and was
increasingly hoity-toity, but Willie and Tad were sure
to be following behind their Mama, messing around with
ornaments, staring at people, ringing the bells, skidding
along marble floors or sliding down mahogany banisters.
Sometimes they brought pet goats or turkeys into the
house, and once Tad set up a lemonade stand in the hall.
Mrs Lincoln often had relatives staying with her, and
miscellaneous cronies of hers, not all very suitable,
haunted the Executive Mansion.

Remarkably varied visitors were welcomed to this
household. General Tom Thumb, the most celebrated
of all midgets, and his new wife were given a honeymoon
party in the East Room (*Robert Lincoln*: 'No, mother, I
do not propose to assist in entertaining Tom Thumb.
My notions of duty, perhaps, are somewhat different
from yours'). Hole in the Day, chief of the Chippewa
Indians, was entertained to tea. Hermann the Great Magician gave a performance (*The Great Magician*: 'And now,
Mr President, for my next trick, kindly hand me your
handkerchief.' *The President*: 'You've got me now, I ain't
got one'). Harriet Beecher Stowe was told she was 'the
little woman who wrote the book that made this great
war'. Nathaniel Hawthorne thought the President the
homeliest man he ever saw. Officers and men of the
Russian Fleet put in as part of their goodwill visit to
America (*John Hay*: 'They have vast absorbent powers
and are fiendishly ugly').

Here the appalling Mrs Frémont, wife of a wayward
general, storms in at midnight to defend her husband, and

demands an interview with the President (*The President*: 'Now, at once'). Here hotfoot from England comes Goldwin Smith, Regius Professor of Modern History at Oxford, who is gratified to find in Lincoln 'an English yeoman's solidity of character and good sense, with something added from the enterprising life and sharp habits of the Western Yankee'. And who is that? Nicolai, what does that young woman on the stairs want of me? Only your autograph, sir. In that case come on in, young lady, take a seat, pass me your book – and with a sigh the President writes:

White House, April 19, 1861
Whoever in later times shall see this, and look at the date, will readily excuse the writer for not having indulged in sentiment, or poetry.
With all kind regards for Miss Smith.

A. Lincoln

Foreigners who visited the Lincoln White House thought it a slum or a madhouse: Prince Jérôme Napoleon and his wife Clothilde were appalled to find neither a doorman nor a butler to greet them at the door. In the evening very often, when at last the doors of the Executive Mansion were closed, the band of the United States Marines played in the garden, and Mr and Mrs Lincoln and their children listened from the calm of a balcony; but even then half Washington milled around outside, talking and laughing, shouting bawdy and whistling to the tunes.

★

From my distance of time, from the other side of an ocean, Lincoln seems to have been a President of almost lackadaisical genius. He pottered around a lot. He sat with his feet up on a chair. He wore his trademark hat with an almost theatrical air, as though he might tip it over his eyes, rise languidly to his feet, hitch up his pants and embark upon a barn dance to the fiddle.

Executive Washington was very small. The US Capitol was a mile and a half from the White House, and closer still were the mostly undistinguished buildings that housed the War and Navy departments, the State Department and the Treasury – all the Government offices that were needed in those days. Lincoln had only to walk across his garden to get to them, and he often did, eating an apple on the way, to consult with his Ministers on their own ground, or to hang around the telegraph office at the War Department, looking through the ticker-tapes. Sometimes he took his boys out for a walk, and sometimes, especially after dark, he just walked around by himself, deep in thought. Everyone knew him. In the 1970s there used to be an eccentric who meandered around the White House dressed up as Lincoln, with the same beard and a similar far-away expression on his face. I suspect he was very true to his original: everyone knew him too, and only strangers like me bothered to stare.

Lincoln was never aloof or inaccessible. When he drove across town in his carriage he frequently raised his hat or waved to passers-by; at Riggs Bank on Pennsylvania Avenue they showed me a facsimile of a cheque made out in his handwriting, drawn on his personal account, to an indigent of the sidewalk, 'The Coloured Man with One Leg'. At official receptions he shook every hand with equal warmth; he once kept an entire reception line waiting for five minutes while a guest shared a comic story with him. Often he visited wounded men in the hospitals, and he made a point of inspecting new regiments when they arrived in the capital, taking the salute at parades and always finding time to talk to the men. Once, walking down the ranks of a Pennsylvania unit, he was pulled up short to find a seventeen-year-old infantryman considerably taller than he was himself. The President stood there astonished. The boy was rigid at attention. The whole battalion looked to its front while the President, as one hyper-extension sufferer to another, offered the private some specialist medical advice – to avoid all alcohol, pies and pastry, and to go to sleep with his head lower than his chest.

Often the city saw its Chief Executive on his way to the Soldiers' Home, a military convalescent place five miles north of the White House, on high ground almost at the Maryland border. There was a cottage orné in its grounds which the Lincolns used as a family retreat, especially in the hot weather. The Soldiers' Home is still there, a place of retirement for 4,000 ex-service men and women, and on the edge of it, rather overwhelmed by its institutional structures, Anderson Cottage survives as an administrative office. It is a pretty little structure, the sort of mock-haven that European princesses built for themselves in the purlieus of monstrous palaces, with wide eaves, bargeboarding, a trellissed veranda and a picturesque superfluity of chimneys. The Lincolns loved it. In the 1860s the Soldiers' Home consisted only of a single two-storey building with a tower; from the cottage they could look with relief across trees and woods, where squirrels and chipmunks abounded and the boys loved to play, to see the White House festering in the humid flats below.

One can easily reconstruct Abe's frequent journeys to this merciful refuge. His route lay up Vermont Avenue, which starts at Lafayette Square directly outside the White House, and even now fairly soon descends into ordinariness. Up the street at a slow trot, past the offices of the *Washington Post*, past the Ramada Plaza Hotel, clatters and clangs his little cortège: a lieutenant of the 11th New York Cavalry, twenty troopers riding two by two, carrying their sabres upright at the shoulder, and hemmed in safely among them the President in an open barouche, dressed all in black, dustily, with his tall hat on his head – a thoughtful, incongruous figure among the tossing horsemen. Sometimes Tad rides with them, on his pony. Sometimes a three-legged dog tags along. Occasionally they turn off momentarily into K Street, and the Secretary of War comes out of his front door for a brief consultation. Once they meet a regiment marching the other way, and Lincoln stops his carriage to ask a soldier what it is. 'It's a regiment,' says the man without turning his head. 'I know that,' says the President. 'I want to know what regiment it is.' 'Pennsylvania,' the soldier grunts, totally unimpressed by the cavalcade with its sabres surrounding the President of the United States, and 'Ah well,' says Lincoln, greatly amused, 'drive on, at least he didn't take us for royalty!'

Walt Whitman the poet often saw the little squadron pass. He was working as an orderly at a military hospital in the city, and living in lodgings on L Street. In time the President came to recognize him, watching from the sidewalk there, and courteously bowed.

'I have never dictated events,' Lincoln said. 'Events have dictated me.' But if his approach to the Presidency seemed fatalistic, it was really profoundly studied. He was an ambiguous figure still. Lord Lyons the British Ambassador, whose embassy was a few hundred yards from the White House, met him often and was apparently not especially impressed. W. H. Russell, correspondent of the London *Times*, was sorry for him – 'this poor President! . . . He runs from one house to another, armed with plans, papers, reports, recommendations, sometimes good-humoured, never angry, occasionally dejected, and always a little fussy.' Charles Francis Adams, chosen by Lincoln to be US Minister in London, found him shabby, slouchy and discourteous. Even his closest colleagues often underestimated him, and public opinion about him vacillated, largely according to the fortunes of his armies in the field. His opinion of himself as President seems to have vacillated too – sometimes he thought the burden too great for him to bear.

Gradually it dawned upon him, though, and upon his colleagues and rivals too, that he was the only man who could undertake the Presidency at that moment, in such circumstances. He was not vindictive. He was willing always to learn, or to change his mind. He was experienced and skilled in compromise and persuasion. He

moved shrewdly and cautiously, often keeping his policies to himself as a lawyer conceals his arguments. He
was irreplaceable, and little by little this truth was realized
by his supporters, his opponents, his generals, his armies
and the public. He was one of a kind – unhomogenizable!
If he were to go, there was nobody of the same shape
and stature to fill the gap. His crude Western origins, so
often scorned, began to be seen as an asset. Charles Adams
was to become one of his most admiring supporters, and
James Russell Lowell thought Americans should rejoice
that their leader was 'out of the very earth, un-ancestored,
unprivileged, unknown'.

Lincoln said himself that the task he faced was harder
than anything Washington was up against. From first to
last his Presidency was a balancing act. His principal
opponents were the extreme abolitionists, mostly within
his own party, who thought he never went far enough;
the opposition Democrats, who thought he went much
too far; and miscellaneous political discontents who
merely wanted him out of the way. He disarmed some
of his most formidable critics by appointing them to
his Cabinet, including all his four main rivals for the
Presidency, from both parties. Some who began as surrep-
titious competitors ended up as faithful lieutenants. The
Democrat Edwin Stanton, an old enemy of the Illinois
law courts who had once spoken of Lincoln's 'painful
imbecility', became a loyal Secretary of War. William
Seward had been Lincoln's opponent in the Republican
convention at Chicago, and set out at first to be a kind
of von Papen, a stealthy power behind the throne; but
he came generously to recognize Lincoln's supremacy,

and was an affectionate Secretary of State throughout his Presidency. Lincoln kept some of the pro-slavery factions quiet by repeatedly denying that he wanted to abolish slavery out of hand, only hoped that it would fade away as an anachronism; he did his best with the fierce abolitionists by declaring over and over again his unbounded opposition to the idea of slavery, and to the Slave Power. He bore no resentments, not out of altruism but because he 'never thought it paid'.

He consulted his Cabinet frequently, but did not really want anybody's advice: once he had become President of the United States, he was his own man, and he steered his own course of authority. From the start he showed an unexpected ruthlessness. There was plenty of opposition to the war within the Northern States, from politicians, journalists, churchmen and commerçants doing business with the South. During his first months in office Congress was in recess, but to deal with such subversion Lincoln suspended habeas corpus by Presidential decree. The Chief Justice of the Supreme Court objected that the British Crown itself, that tyrannical old bugbear, had never exercised such power over its people, but Lincoln pleaded military necessity, and in the first six months of the war at least 850 US citizens were imprisoned without charge. People with long memories remembered his tribe of eagles speech, but 'extreme tenderness of the citizen's liberty,' he expostulated, 'might make the Government itself to go to pieces.' Before his Presidency was done he was to imprison thousands more, besides instituting the first American draft and the original American income tax.

Another disturbing political difficulty throughout the war was the existence of the four slave States on the border – Delaware, Kentucky, Maryland and Missouri – which had declined to secede with the rest of the South. Kentucky, Lincoln's native State, in particular obsessed him – he would like to have God on his side, he said, but he *must* have Kentucky. (Perhaps his own complex loyalties were involved: seven men from the Todd family of Lexington fought with the Confederate armies.) The border States were neutrals of a sort, and Lincoln was preoccupied with the problem of keeping them that way. He failed to persuade them to accept the idea of *gradual* compensated emancipation, which would come 'gently as the dews from heaven', and fell back upon the old reassurances that he was not a rabid abolitionist, only an abominator of the slavery principle. This equilibrium was always at the back of his mind – between the righteous indignation of the abolitionists and the furious resentment of the slave-holders – and it meant that for the first years of the civil war he was unable to make a high moral cause of it. The war was being fought, he repeatedly claimed, only because the Constitution did not allow individual States to secede from the Republic – hardly an inspiration for a crusade.

For much of the time he was intensely unpopular in the country at large, and a nadir was reached very early in his term. On 21 July 1861, the fourth month of his Presidency, his armies suffered a terrible defeat at Manassas in Virginia, only 20 miles from Washington. It was the first pitched battle of the war. Lincoln had himself urged his commanders to attack the Confederate forces, and so confident was everyone of victory that hundreds of Washingtonians went out in holiday mood to watch the fighting, equipped with opera glasses and picnic hampers like the spectators riding out from Brussels to Waterloo. By the end of the day 2,986 Union soldiers were killed, wounded or missing, and the Northerners, soldiers, spectators and all, were in headlong retreat back to Washington. Next morning the streets of the capital were desolate with filthy, exhausted and disheartened soldiers, some in columns, some solitary stragglers, often without their weapons, blistered, sweaty and powder-grimed, many of them falling to the ground in side-alleys and sleeping where they lay. 'The dream of humanity,' wrote Whitman of the scene, 'the vaunted Union we thought so strong, so impregnable – lo! it seems already smashed like a China plate.' A storm of bitter contumely burst around Lincoln's head, when the meaning of this tragic scene sunk home. He had never been criticized like this before. He was an incompetent traitor, a hypocrite, a hideous baboon who ought to be exhibited at Barnum's circus. Vicious cartoons filled the newspapers. Hostile politicians threw abuse. After five months in office, he wondered why anybody would want the job.

Here we see him, nevertheless, going to have his picture taken. On Pennsylvania Avenue there still stands the brown brick house which, during the 1860s, housed the studio of Matthew Brady, the most celebrated photographer of the day. It is only a block or two from the White House, and if we lean against the wall on the other side of the street we may fancy Lincoln arriving for a session with the master or one of his assistants. I like to suppose he walked down there, tipping his hat to passers-by and responding to the friendlier greetings of the sidewalk – 'Good day to you, Mr President, sir!', 'God bless you Mr President!' At an upstairs window a face appears, watching for his arrival, and the moment he approaches the door it is opened for him. A cheerful young man takes his hat and precedes him up the steep stairs to Brady's studio on the third floor, where he indulges in his usual badinage with the photographers. If they take him standing up, will they get him all in? They want him to look natural, do they? Well, that's the last thing *he* wants to look! Has he ever told them the story of how he set out to find somebody uglier than himself? How will this new pose go down with the Cabinet, or old Jeff Davis down in Richmond, or Mary, or most important of all, the electorate?

For while it was a chore for the President, it was a vital one. He had long grasped the political importance of image. He sat for more than 100 photographs in his time, and became the most familiar figure of all the American Presidents of history – whole books have been published purely of his photographic portraits. He was an unassuming, but not I think a modest man. He always talked of his plainness, but I suspect he protested too much: he surely knew that his unmistakable face was one of his great assets, and he was never indifferent to publicity – in his pockets when he died they found eight laudatory press cuttings. Honest Abe was a politician still, a master of political artifice, and he was alive to all the tricks of his trade. When Charles Adams called on him that day, before leaving for London, Lincoln said not a word about his mission, merely calling over his shoulder to Seward that he had made up his mind about the Chicago post office appointment . . .

Nor was he any less wily than most of his colleagues. He wriggled and back-tracked and double-talked and distributed patronage with the best (or worst) of them. In 1864, the third year of his term, he had to fight another Presidential election, and all the odds seemed to be stacked against him. The war was going badly and his public standing was very low. The Press in general professed to despise him, and loaded him with wildly varied abuse: trying to answer all their accusations, one of his supporters commented, would be like asking a virgin to prove her chastity. The Democrats' candidate was the popular General George McClellan, and their spin-doctors fought a venomous campaign, with racism rather than slavery at the core of it. They accused Lincoln of deliberately encouraging miscegenation, and hinted that he might have Negro blood himself. 'Filthy black niggers,' said the New York *Freeman's Journal*, 'greasy, sweaty and disgusting, now jostle with white people . . . even at the President's levees.'

Lincoln almost despaired of winning, but responded with his usual agility. He rid himself of political embarrassments, for a start. 'You have generously said to me more than once,' he wrote to his Postmaster-General, Montgomery Blair, 'that whenever your resignation could be a relief to me, it was at my disposal. That time has come.' He called in all the debts of patronage. He offered James Gordon Bennett of the New York *Herald*, one of his most persistent critics, the post of Minister to France. He saw to it that the Territory of Nevada was admitted to the Union as a State on 31 October, thus ensuring himself another three electoral votes in November. He arranged for soldiers in the field, his strongest supporters, to get home on leave to vote. He tried to avoid major military actions for the time being – heavy casualty lists would lose him votes.

Fortunately almost at that very moment there was a dramatic turn in the fortunes of war, Union forces capturing Atlanta in Georgia and driving the Confederates from the Shenandoah Valley in Virginia. Lincoln won his election hands down, and was elated. 'For such an awkward fellow I am pretty sure-footed,' he said, and he threw a midnight election party at the White House telegraph office, distributing fried oysters with his own hands.

But in the course of his Presidency, it seems to me as it has seemed to many before me, something transcendental happened to Abraham Lincoln. We have been tracing in this book the career of a kind, agreeable, likeable and clever man emerging from the sticks to be caught in the throes of an overriding ambition, with no very lofty aspirations, only a drive for personal success. We have watched him becoming adept at the slippery and not always very honourable devices of the democratic system, and we have seen that even as President of the United States he was still using the political trickery he had learnt on the way up. But once his highest possible worldly ambition had been achieved, his mind appears to have turned to grander ends – in Bertrand Russell's metaphor, to the opening of windows upon 'a wider and less fretful cosmos'.

For one thing this ultra-American patriot cultivated a *weltanschauung*, a world-view. In 1861 the Republic of San Marino made him an honorary citizen. A minute enclave in central Italy, San Marino was one of the world's smallest and most insignificant republics, and I cannot help wondering if Lincoln had ever heard of it before. He expressed his gratitude diplomatically, nevertheless: 'Although your Dominion is small your State is nevertheless one of the most honoured in all history.' Again, when the King of Siam offered the US Government a stock of elephants for breeding purposes, Lincoln replied as to the ambassadorial manner born:

This government would not hesitate to avail itself of so generous an offer if the object were one which could be made practically useful in the present condition of the United States. Our political jurisdiction, however, does not reach a latitude so low as to favour the multiplication of the elephant, and steam on land, as well as on water, has been our best and most efficient agent of transportation in internal commerce ... Meanwhile, wishing Your Majesty a long and happy life, and for the generous and emulous people of Siam the highest possible prosperity, I commend both to the blessing of Almighty God.

For the first time he was now involved in foreign affairs: and so important were relations with other States to the course of his war that he learnt the niceties fast.

Unworldly, untravelled, monolingual, insular in the sense that he knew little about the great world outside the United States, and had seldom seen the open sea, he nevertheless cherished the notion that he was fighting a war on behalf of all mankind. This was his *weltanschauung*: that the US Declaration of Independence, proclaiming all men to have equal rights, had a universal meaning. It 'gave hope to the world for all future time', and the united American democracy that was based upon it was destined to provide a model for all other nations.

In fact he had no very sophisticated measures of comparison. The only foreign country he ever set foot in was Canada. The only history he knew anything about, except the brief history of his own country, was England's, and his command of that was elementary – all he remembered about the English Civil War, he said, was that Charles I had his head cut off. Generally he thought simplistically in terms of Kings and People. Kings were bad, Peoples were good, a view which was later to commend him to Karl Marx, and he was proud that there was 'no smell of royalty' to his White House, an assessment with which Prince Jérôme Napoleon would certainly have agreed. Kings, he said, 'had always been involving and impoverishing their people in wars', and the American Revolution against George III of England had been a revolution on behalf of all the family of man. So in fighting the civil war, too, the American Republic was proclaiming to the whole world the resilience of popular government – so that 'the succeeding millions of free happy people, the world over, shall rise up, and call us blessed, to the latest generations.'

Now he evidently grasped how interdependent governments were, whether monarchies or republics, and what a useful emollient diplomacy might be. Ideology could be set aside in the cause of his world-view, just as Churchill was to swallow his anti-Communist ideals when it came to saving Europe from the Nazis. 'One doesn't like to make a messenger of the King of France,' he said in all seriousness when the exiled pretender to the French throne, the twenty-three-year-old Comte de Paris, arrived at the White House with a dispatch. The Tsar of all the Russias might be the very archetype of autocracy, but nevertheless Lincoln called him, in a diplomatic message, 'the great sovereign whose personal and hereditary friendship for the United States so much endears him to Americans'. He abruptly dismissed Seward's Machiavellian idea of provoking a war with France and Spain, monarchies both, as a means of bringing the Southern States back into national unity. Even those old enemies the British, who often showed an infuriating sympathy for the Southern cause, he treated with careful tact, and he intervened to prevent a conflict with them in 1861. 'One war at a time,' he is supposed to have said when a hot-headed Union navy captain, discovering some Confederate diplomats aboard the British steamer *Trent*, summarily arrested them against all the laws of the sea; like the Duke of Wellington, who said he was never afraid to drop a knee before a foreign grandee if it would help him win a war, Lincoln was not ashamed of appeasement, and he saw to it that the diplomats were released and sent on their way.

Mind you, the Union armies depended for their gun-

powder upon saltpetre from British India, the Comte de
Paris was serving in the Union army, and the reformist
Tsar Alexander II had just given the anti-slavery cause
a boost by emancipating the Russian serfs. American
interests came first, even if they could be interpreted as
being all the world's interests. A dispute arose in 1861
between Spain and the Negro administration of the
Dominican Republic – black libertarians against mon-
archist imperialists – in which the US might well have
involved itself. Lincoln said he was reminded of a conversation between a black preacher and one of his flock.
'There are two roads before you, Joe,' said Josh the
preacher. 'The narrow way leads straight to hell, the
broad way leads to damnation.' Joe was appalled at
the alternatives. 'Josh, you take which road you please,
I'll go *through the wood*' – and just at the moment, Lincoln
said, he felt the same: he would support neither the
Negroes nor the Spaniards, but would take to the woods.

Lincoln once called the Americans the Almighty's
almost chosen people, but he believed that America was
decidedly the chosen land. The democratic principle
was the instrument of providence that made it supreme
among all others, and his idea of democracy was simple.
'As I would not be a *slave*, so I would not be a *master*.'

Lincoln's family brought him much suffering during his
Presidency, and perhaps helped to disillusion him with
the world and its pretensions. His beloved son Willie
died of cholera in 1862. His eldest boy Robert, having
failed fifteen out of sixteen subjects in the Harvard
entrance examination, got in at last and emerged an

unsympathetic bore. Tad, his remaining delight and by then his almost inseparable companion, for the life of him could not learn to write. And there was always Mary . . .

Mary had grown decidedly plump, and had taken to dressing in an ostentatiously girlish manner, with leanings towards blues, magentas and royal purples around the whites of innocence. She loved to wear flowers in her hair, and went in for heaps of lace, lashings of feathers, and furbelows (sixty bows on a dress she was especially fond of). She had not been happy in Washington. Local high society, so much of it Southern, resented her as a renegade Kentuckian, who had abandoned her own cause and even her own family, including its slaves. Political opportunists exploited her. Foreigners mocked her behind her back. Prince Napoleon said she dressed in a tasteless French style and served a bad French dinner. Her chief confidants were her own relatives, on their frequent visits to the capital, and her black seamstress Elizabeth Keckley – surrogate for her black mammies of old? Her chief consolations were her children, her clothes and her paranoically uncontrollable passion for shopping.

Perhaps when Willie died, the second of her sons to go, something cracked inside the poor woman's mind. She connived with a crooked gardener to cheat the Treasury, she grossly overspent her official allowance, she enabled a disreputable Frenchman to steal Presidential papers, she ran up preposterous bills at the most expensive stores in Washington, Boston and New York – in one month she bought eighty-four pairs of gloves. She repapered the White House with wallpaper imported from France, and equipped it with gold cutlery and a new chinaware set of 560 pieces. She accepted expensive gifts – horses, furs – in return for arranging Presidential favours. She allegedly slept with a superannuated hotel manager. She was not a wicked woman, and she loved her husband with a childishly possessive pride, but she had taken to wandering beyond the boundaries of normal civilized behaviour. She thought her Abraham 'almost a monomaniac on the subject of honesty' . . .

'Miserable man!' wrote Herndon, who always detested Mary. 'Lincoln had to do things which he knew were out of place in order to keep his wife's fingers out of his hair.' Even his enemies pitied him his marital problems, and sometimes his patience was all too visibly strained by Mary's illogical excesses. A famously dreadful embarrassment occurred when she accompanied him on a visit to his armies encamped beside the James River, some 50 miles south of Washington. She arrived late and bad-tempered for a Presidential review one day in time to see her husband riding down the ranks accompanied by Mrs Edward Ord, wife of one of his generals, mounted on a splendid bay and wearing a gloriously dashing hat with a Robin Hood feather on it. This spectacle infuriated her, and after the parade she fell upon her Abraham like a tigress, in full public hearing. 'He bore it,' said an officer who was present, 'as Christ might have done, with an expression of pain and sadness that cut one to the heart': yet still he cherished her, made excuses for her, tried to cover up for her, and once assured a guest at a White House reception that 'my wife is as handsome as she was when she was a girl and I, a poor nobody then, fell in love with her . . . and have never fallen out.'

By the nature of things Lincoln was preoccupied with race. Half a century before, as a boy at a backwoods school, he had read in a textbook called *The Kentucky Preceptor* a discussion on the subject 'Which has the more right to complain, the Indian or the Negro?' According to Herndon he took a deep interest in 'this grave subject', and perhaps he sometimes remembered *The Kentucky Preceptor* now that the subject had become far graver still.

For the moment the Native Americans – the Red Indians as they were called in his time – were complaining less, standing as they did on the edge of the civil war. Lincoln never seems to have been altogether at ease with this disturbing minority. His paternal grandfather, another Abraham, had been killed in an Indian ambush in Kentucky in the previous century. He himself had gone to war against the Sauk and Fox Indians, and if he never exchanged shots with them, he never forgot the horror of seeing five scalped white corpses on someone else's battlefield. Thirty years later, with the civil war raging, he was obliged to send a force to put down a brutal Sioux rising in Minnesota, and authorized the hanging of thirty-eight tribesmen, the largest mass execution in American history. No wonder he seemed uncomfortable when Indian delegations visited the White House. At worst he talked to them in stilted pidgin English, at best he was patronizing, speaking of the pale-faced people, and the great round ball that was the world, and the unfortunate tendency of 'our red brethren to fight and kill each other'. In a photograph I have before me now a feathered and tomahawked group of visiting Indians look bemused, as well they might, considering that the pale-faces had killed at least 100,000 of each other during the previous three years.

But of course it was the place of the black man in American society that lay at the root of all his anxieties. He remained a man of his times on the issue. If it was politic enough for him to declare the wickedness of the Peculiar Institution, it was by no means politically advantageous to claim that the black man was the white man's equal. Nor did he claim it. Hardly anyone else did either, on either side of the Atlantic – even Harriet Beecher Stowe scarcely implied that Uncle Tom might properly have married the Master's daughter! In the Douglas debates Lincoln had been careful to deride the very notion of racial equality, and even during the war he distanced the preservation of the Union from the cause of the black people: 'If I could save the Union without freeing any slaves I would do it; and if I could save it by freeing some and leaving others alone, I would also do that.'

'All men are created equal,' it seemed, did not mean exactly that after all. Warily though Lincoln trod the ethnic path, he was specific in claiming that the races were inherently *un*equal, and well into his Presidency he was still maintaining that the solution to the racial problem was the repatriation of black people to Africa, or their relocation somewhere else. Colombia was one suggestion, an island off Haiti another, an enclave in Texas a third. As an Illinois soldier wrote home from the

front: 'I am not in favor of freeing the Negroes and
leaving them to run free among us nether is Sutch the
intention of Old Abe but we will Send them off and
colonize them.' When a delegation of black leaders came
to see him at the White House, Lincoln told them
just that, not altogether to their satisfaction. Frederick
Douglass the famous black activist said that the Negro
people were only the *step*-children of Father Abraham,
'by force of circumstances and necessity'.

Douglass also said, nevertheless, that Lincoln was the
first great man he had ever met who 'in no single instance
reminded me of the difference between himself and
myself, of the difference of colour'. Whatever his reasoning on race, Lincoln was as instinctively decent to black
people as he was to white. Returning one day from the
Soldiers' Home, he came across a party of slaves who
had escaped from the South – 'contrabands', they were
called – and legend says he dismounted to join them,
with tears in his eyes, as they sang spirituals through the
summer evening. It must surely sometimes have troubled
his conscience that the North's war aims did not include
the compulsory liberation of the slaves, yet he consistently
dismissed the idea. It would be constitutionally illegal
and it would antagonize the slave States of the border,
who might well be pushed into secession. When after
two years of war he changed his mind, he claimed that
military necessity alone compelled him: it was certainly
true that the Southern armies had the advantage in morale
of fighting in a personal, heartfelt cause, whereas the
Northerners fought only out of duty or conventional
patriotism. Whatever the reason, Lincoln's eventual

Proclamation of Emancipation meant that the Civil War was no longer just a gigantic political squabble, but a moral crusade at last.

It was a personal decision. At first most of his Cabinet were astonished, when he told them what he planned to do, and some of them disagreed. Lincoln wrote and rewrote the proclamation, sometimes while waiting for news from the front in the War Department telegraph room, sometimes in the privacy of the Soldiers' Home. After the event cartoonists of North and South depicted the process: the one side presenting a diabolically plotting Lincoln surrounded by satanic talismans, with celebratory pictures of slave revolts on the walls of the White House, the other showing him meditating amidst a noble litter of maps, memorials, petitions and legal documents, with a Holy Bible on his knee. The war was going disastrously for the North then, defeat seemed perfectly possible, and on Seward's advice Lincoln postponed the emancipation announcement until the news took a turn for the better, in case it was seen as a measure of desperation. In July 1862, the North at last won a moderate success at Antietam, in Maryland, and on 22 September the President presented a draft proclamation to his Ministers in the Cabinet Room at the White House.

We know from personal memoirs how the meeting went, and we can imagine what it looked like from one of the most famous of Lincoln paintings, by the New York artist F. B. Carpenter, who spent some months in the White House reconstructing the event. In slightly unlikely poses, so as to show all their faces, the Ministers are assembled around their President, who sits in a tall-backed

Windsor chair: Seward (State), Stanton (War), Salmon Chase (Treasury), Montgomery Blair (Postmaster-General), Gideon Welles (Navy), Caleb Smith (Interior), Edward Bates (Attorney-General), attended by symbolical accessories – law books, maps, scrolled documents. Carpenter has disposed the men according to their importance, Seward, Stanton and Welles sitting close to the President, Chase standing at his shoulder, the others in the background. They already knew more or less what to expect that day, and if the artist's interpretation is anything to go by (Lincoln thought the picture 'as good as it can be made') were not unduly excited by the significance of the occasion.

Anyway Lincoln, easing himself comfortably in his chair, put on his spectacles and began by reading the assembled Cabinet a comical passage from a book he was currently enjoying. It was Artemus Ward's *A High-Handed Outrage at Utica*, and had been sent to him by the author. How he laughed, I like to fancy, until the chair creaked and he had to wipe his eyes with his handkerchief, as he read them the bit where the hero bashes in the head of Judas in a wax tableau of the Last Supper, to demonstrate that 'Judas Iscarrot can't show himself in Utiky with impunerty by a darn site'! Most of the Ministers managed no more than a smile in response – Stanton and Chase not even that – and the President chaffed them for their lack of appreciation. 'Why don't you laugh, gentlemen? If I didn't laugh I should die, and you need this medicine as much as I do . . .'

Then to business. He could now redeem the promise, Lincoln told them, which he had long before made to himself ('and to my God,' the sanctimonious Chase thought he heard him add). The time for emancipation had come. From New Year's Day, 1863, anyone held as a slave within any State or part of a State in rebellion against the Union Government would be 'then, thenceforward and forever free'. The Cabinet members were not much surprised by now – they knew he had only been waiting for some change in the military situation – and Lincoln told them that while he was not at all sure he was doing the right thing, his mind was made up. He would welcome criticisms only of the proclamation's text.

There was, it seems, no rush to offer amendments. It was a *fait accompli* really. Lincoln dropped some clauses which might be seen as an incitement to slave rebellion. He put in one encouraging former slaves to join the Union armed forces. At Chase's urging he added a final invocation to 'the gracious favour of Almighty God'. So the meeting ended – one of the most fateful Cabinet meetings of American history – and when a couple of days later Lincoln was cheered by crowds celebrating his preliminary Proclamation of Emancipation, he told them: 'I can only trust in God I have made no mistake.'

Many have argued that there was no splendour to the Proclamation at all. Pure expedience, it was said, was its only motive. It was an ultimatum to the Southern States either to return to the Union by 1 January 1863, or to lose all their slaves in the end. It was a diplomatic measure, to assuage opinion in Europe. It was a shifty bit of policy – only two months had passed, after all, since Lincoln had declared the maintenance of the Union with or without slavery to be his paramount purpose. It was a dull and legalistic piece of writing with 'the moral grandeur of a bill of lading'. Since it applied only to territories under the control of the Confederacy, it meant that Abe had freed all the slaves except the ones he *could* free. Among Confederates it was predictably greeted with mingled contempt, venom and outrage, for they recognized at once that the war purposes of the Union would now embrace the complete subjugation of the South and its cherished institutions – *delenda est Carthago*. Jefferson Davis himself called it one of the 'most execrable measures in the history of guilty man'.

But the Emancipation Proclamation led before long to the 13th Amendment of the Constitution, which in 1865 outlawed the Peculiar Institution from all parts of the United States once and for all. Whatever Lincoln's motives, in a way it was to liberate him, too, and turn yesterday's Railsplitter into tomorrow's Great Emancipator.

Did he find religion during these terrible years? He certainly attended services at the New York Avenue Presbyterian Church, but perhaps he was merely doing his duty by the nation whose motto was 'In God We Trust'. In the last year of his life he told a friend that he was 'profitably engaged in reading the Bible', but perhaps it was more as literature than as theology. Certainly he referred to God far more often than he used to – or at least to the Almighty, a no less nebulous abstraction – and he was more easily induced to add a note of piety to his public addresses. In 1863 he established a national

Thanksgiving Day in an announcement that was one long unctuous cliché, full of references to the most gracious gifts of the Most High, to our beneficent Father who dwelleth in the heavens, ascriptions, deliverances and recent blessings (i.e. the recent deaths or mutilations of many thousands of US citizens). Some people thought he turned to religion after Willie's death, the saddest blow of his life. Every Thursday he shut himself away for a time in the boy's bedroom, mourning or communing – he seems to have tinkered with spiritualism, one of Mary's passions, and went so far as to allow séances in the White House. There was a story that the Emancipation Proclamation itself was written on the tranced advice of a well-known medium, Nettie Colburn Maynard, to whom he gave a job in the Department of the Interior.

He never lost his pagan sense of fatalism, or his taste for the gloomy poetry of predestination, a new favourite being Oliver Wendell Holmes' 'The Last Leaf':

> *The mossy marbles rest*
> *On the lips that he has pressed*
> *In their bloom;*
> *And the names he loved to hear*
> *Have been carved for many a year*
> *On the tomb.*

I suspect he remained a sceptical theist, like most people becoming rather less sceptical as the years passed. I take with a pinch of salt reports by pious visitors to the White House that Lincoln joined them in spontaneous prayer. When he was photographed reading a book to Tad, he was at pains to make it known that the book was *not* a Bible, and when a lecturing Quaker urged him to free the slaves, on the grounds that God had chosen him to do the job, he 'suggested for her consideration the question whether, if it be true that the Lord has appointed me to do the work she has indicated, it is not probable that He would have communicated knowledge of the fact to me as well as to her.' He told a moralizing Illinois evangelist, who said he was bringing the Word of the Lord from Chicago to the White House, that it seemed an odd route for the Word to take. It struck him as bizarre, as it must most rational thinkers, that both sides in a war prayed to the same God with equal sincerity and conviction – 'both *may* be, and one *must* be wrong.'

But Lincoln was something of a mystic always, perhaps accepting the all-embracing Unitarian trust in a Fatherhood of God and a Brotherhood of Man. He was essentially a *nice* man. Academic historians cannot allow themselves such flip idiomatic judgements, but to an outsider like me that seems about the truth of it. He was a *nice* man. He could be scheming, irritable, disingenuous, but he was never pompous or overbearing. Who but an Abe Lincoln would have been found lying on a sofa in the White House with a telescope propped between his big feet, watching the Potomac ships go by? What other President would have been so heart-rendingly fond of the little scamp Tad as to take him to official functions and parades, even into Cabinet meetings or on Presidential visits to the war zone? Would any other Chief Executive be given a present of *kittens* by his Secretary of State? On a Saturday midnight in 1864 Nicolai and

Hay were working in their office at the White House
when the door opened and a laughing Lincoln entered,
carrying a book. He looked inexpressibly comical, in a
short nightshirt that hung around his long legs, so Hay
thought, 'like the tail feathers of an enormous ostrich'.
Why had the sixteenth President of the United States
got up from his bed and come pacing down the corridors
of the Executive Mansion in the middle of the night, at
a time when the fate of his country hung upon his
decisions? Only to share with his two young secretaries
the pleasure of a funny caricature by Thomas Hood.

   Mary perceptively thought his religion was 'a kind of
poetry in his nature': Karl Marx, from the other side of
the Atlantic, saw him simply as 'one of the few men
who became great while remaining good'. We would
probably judge him good too, I think, if we could
accompany a pair of overseas visitors to his office at the
White House one Saturday evening, when the crowds
have dispersed. Mr Hay, having welcomed us at the head
of the stairs, leads us to the Presidential quarters, knocks
upon the door and introduces us: 'Mr President, Mr
and Mrs Smith from Liverpool in England.' Lincoln is
sprawling in a chair in his socks, one of which has a hole
in it, with a pair of kittens scrambling all over him. He
rises to his feet at once, slips with some difficulty into
his slippers, pushes the kittens off and crosses the room
to shake our hands. 'From Liverpool in England, my
word,' he says, 'a long way to come, my word. Welcome
to Washington, Mr Smith, Ma'am, albeit not at the
happiest moment of our history. I have been told a great
deal about your tremendous city – all those ships, all

those docks – my goodness, so far we can offer nothing to match it – but give us time, give us time!'

He takes us to chairs by the fire – 'I love an open fire, I always have one to home' – and apologizes for the kittens – 'Mrs Lincoln sometimes says I should be rid of them, they tear the furniture so, but I'd rather swallow my buckthorne chair than throw the little critters out.' Settling down himself, stretching out his long legs for the kittens to climb over, upon a kneeler embroidered with the American eagle, he rings for tea. 'Tea for you Ma'am, am I right? And for you Sir, I fear you may wish for something stronger, but alas we have no spirits here, and can offer you only good Potomac water. No? Tea for you too? Then I will join you.'

He sighs, rather ruefully. 'You will pardon me my manners Ma'am, I know. My dear wife says I am sadly uncouth, but I have been having a difficult day, and my legs are grumbling rather. By this time of the week I'm badgered about to death. And when I'm tired, I must tell you, I can be as savage as a wildcat!' But no, his conversation is slow, easy and considerate. Now and then, as we have been warned, he puts down his teacup, places his elbows on the table, rests his face between his hands, and beginning, 'That rather reminds me . . .', embarks upon one of his homespun back-country tales, hardly restraining his own laughter as he does so. Once, after a moment of silence, he asks us what we think of this terrible war, this sinful war between brothers, to which we can do no more than murmur sympathetically, having ourselves (as we say) recently lost some dear ones in our own war of secession, the Indian Mutiny. When

Tad bursts into the room, with a hoop and a cockatoo in a cage, he laughingly introduces us, gives him a cake and a few crumbs for the bird, and unsuccessfully tries to shoo him out again.

Never mind, it is time for us to go anyway. Mr Lincoln sees us to the door, Tad hanging on his coat-sleeve, and shakes our hands over a last anecdote – 'saying goodbye always puts me in mind of an old woodman back in Illinois, who used to say to his dog . . .' He calls for Hay in the room next door, and asks him to see us safely back to Willard's. 'Did you ever hear about my own arrival at Willard's, by the way, back in 1861? Did the newspapers report all that in Liverpool? No? Well, it was like this . . .' But young Mr Hay smilingly detaches us, and the President leaves us at the door chuckling still, but looking homesick about the eyes, as though he is about to return to hospital or boarding school.

'What did you make of our tycoon?' asks John Hay as we leave the building, but we hardly know what to say. 'Is he really up to the strain?' says Mr Smith, but Mrs Smith just sighs. 'Poor man,' she says, 'poor dear man.'

Throughout the four years of war Abraham Lincoln was in sole command. All responsibility was his. Even in its truncated condition, by 1865 his Republic was one of the great Powers of the earth, a towering industrial giant with the largest of all armies and navies. The demands of his job were incessant and almost unbearable – the decisions he had to make, generally all on his own, the letters he had to write, often in his own hand, the supplicants he had to deal with, the campaigns he had to authorize, the executions he must order or rescind, the petty political tasks that were still his duty, the never-ending, never-relaxing stream of functions he had to attend, the awful burden of responsibility, the tragic sense of guilt, shame or regret that inevitably oppresses the wager of war and the commander of battles. The ghosts of a hundred thousand soldiers haunted him, and the tears of all their mothers and widows.

Nothing was easy for him, not even sticking to his own convictions. There were times when he wavered in his determination to win the war, and toyed with the idea of an accommodation with the South. Hints of treason, whispers of treachery disturbed him. Defeatists exasperated him, generals disappointed him, colleagues conspired against him, hostile newspaper comment depressed him, more than one old friend was killed in action and through it all ran the thread of his family misfortunes – a wife, not quite normal, who was a running embarrassment to him, one son dead in babyhood, one in boyhood, one without much empathy for him and one with a speech impediment and a backward mind. 'When this is over, I tell my boy Tad, we will go back to the farm, when I was happier as a boy when I dug potatoes at 25 cents a day than I am now. I tell him I will buy him a mule and a pony and he shall have a little garden, in a field all his own.'

At first some had supposed he would be a malleable President. Edward Bates the Attorney-General wrote of him in 1861: 'The President's an excellent man, and in the main wise: but he lacks *will* and *purpose*, and, I greatly fear, he has not the power to *command*.' But as the years went by Lincoln's strength became apparent to all. It was not a rock-like strength. Even his sycophants never called him rock-like. On the contrary, he remained essentially flexible in his thinking. Harriet Beecher Stowe thought him like a tough bit of rope, which might swing from side to side, but would never break. It never did, either, but it certainly frayed. Constant shifts of tactic and response, frequent self-doubts, evasions and pretences, the keeping of secrets and the marshalling of arguments – three years of this wore Lincoln down. For weeks at a time he could not sleep. He lost twenty pounds during his time at the White House. He lost much of his earthy *joie de vivre*, too, and his hearty laughter was not so often heard. The innumerable photographs taken of him during his White House years show an unmistakable decline towards despair, the face ever more lined, the eyes ever less sparkling, the mouth beginning to appear, in a man in his late fifties, like that of a man of seventy. Carpenter the painter thought it 'the saddest face I ever saw'.

Abraham Lincoln's was a martyrdom waiting to happen, and his portraits show it. For myself I do not much like the look of him in his youth or young manhood, with his hair smarmed down and his eyes sharp. Even when he had grown his beard and assumed his final persona, there often seems to me something too calculating about his face, something almost sly. But as the decades passed, and time after time he went down to Brady's studio for another sitting, to my mind a true beauty entered his features. A sad, resigned kindness cleared his eyes and mouth of cunning then, and he began to look as though all the world's sufferings, all his own anxieties, had scoured any resentment from his soul. In the very last photograph of all, taken on 10 April 1865, when he was approaching the triumphant climax of his Presidency, his enemies on their knees before him, his people adoring at his back, all his policies vindicated — at this marvellous moment of victory Abe Lincoln looked perfectly ready for death.

Five

'Get down!' – Commander-in-Chief – a mixed bag of generals – visiting the troops – dealing with Virginia – Berkeley – Gettysburg – City Point – the last foray

Near the Maryland line in Washington, almost within sight of the Soldiers' Home, stands one of the forts so hastily thrown up to defend the capital during the civil war. It is called Fort Stevens, and although its masonry structures are gone its earthworks are in fine condition, 20 or 30 feet high, built in a rough half-circle facing north-west across the outer suburbs. Some guns are still *in situ*. When I was there one sunny day a party of rollicking black children was enjoying a picnic on the well-mown green, supervised by two patient ladies in bright cottons. There used to be a Methodist church on the site, long since removed across the road, and Mrs

Elizabeth ('Aunt Betty') Thomas, a well-known member of the black community, had a house there until in 1863 German-born soldiers of a Pennsylvania regiment pulled it down in order to extend the fort's magazine.

On 11 July 1864, 14,000 Confederate troops under the command of General Jubal A. Early approached this stronghold from the north, probing and testing the defences of Washington. They had crossed the Potomac out of Virginia into Maryland, and were now only eight or nine miles from the White House. The Confederates had never entered the District of Columbia before, and extra Union forces were rushed across the city to face them – by then the war was going the Union's way, but the fall of the capital might well alter its whole course again. Lincoln was hurried away from Anderson Cottage, where he had been staying, and a ship was made ready to sail him downriver if the worst came to the worst. He scoffed at these precautions, and instead insisted on going to Fort Stevens to see things for himself. There, on the evening of 12 July, unmistakeable with his tall hat, black suit and angular posture, he climbed the ramparts and stood there for all to see looking towards the enemy positions. The fort was under heavy fire. A man next to Lincoln was wounded and fell, but the President still stood there, impassive. 'Get down, you damned fool!' cried a young officer, and presently Lincoln withdrew, protesting, out of the line of fire.

It was his battle-baptism, the only time a serving American President has been under enemy gunfire. A plaque on the rampart pictures Lincoln in his hat with the wounded soldier falling backwards at his side, and the occasion has gone into fable. The officer who shouted at the President is said to have been Oliver Wendell Holmes II, son of the author of 'The Last Leaf'. Among the enemy forces, over there beyond the trees, was General John Breckinridge, former Vice-President of the United States and an old acquaintance of Lincoln's. General Early claimed he could hardly move a regiment without being spotted from the tower of the Soldiers' Home. And the folk-memory has not forgotten 'Aunt Betty' Thomas. Still disconsolate about the loss of her house – since the Pennsylvanians spoke no English, she had not understood what was happening – she was sitting under a sycamore tree weeping quietly one evening when a tall stranger approached her to say: 'It is hard, but you shall reap great reward.'

Who but Father Abraham?

One might surmise that like General Gordon at Khartoum, if in less pressing circumstances, at Fort Stevens Lincoln was deliberately courting death. After three years of war the enemy was at the very gates of his capital, and perhaps he felt he had simply had enough. Why else, as Captain Holmes might have said, be such a bloody fool? My own feeling, though, is that Lincoln probably went up the ramparts out of inquisitive bravado. He wanted to know what it would be like. Although everything about his character suggests the man of peace – had he not foresworn hunting after shooting that poor turkey? – history has ironically decreed that he should be remembered above all as a war leader, the only US President (so far) to serve his term of office entirely in wartime. More ironically still, Lincoln could well be considered one of the fathers of modern warfare.

Of course he was horrified by the slaughter and the suffering, on a scale the modern world had never known before, but like many another he was fascinated despite himself by the art and the craft of war. I suspect he liked the swagger of armies, especially the free-and-easy style of American soldiering then, not so long descended from the raggedy panache of the Minutemen. It was the Confederate commander Robert E. Lee who, surveying the course of one of his bloody assaults, remarked to an aide, 'It's a good thing war is so terrible, or we should get too fond of it,' and his aide Thomas 'Stonewall' Jackson who was heard to murmur, on the eve of a desperate engagement, *'delicious excitement'*; but Abraham Lincoln may well have felt rather the same way. War was at once simpler, more theatrical and more honest than politics, and he threw himself into its conduct as wholeheartedly as Churchill did in the next century. Restrained only by a joint congressional committee on the conduct of the war, he never forgot that he was not only President of the United States, but also Commander-in-Chief of all its forces.

He borrowed the works of Clausewitz from the Congressional Library. With his lifelong interest in rivers, canals and railroads he studied the techniques of military communications. He concerned himself with weaponry, both naval and military: he tried out new guns, he inspected new ships, he eagerly interviewed inventors who brought their ideas to the White House. He followed the course of the struggle in detail, and spent more time in the War Department telegraph room than anywhere else except the White House itself. He frequently questioned the plans of his generals, and offered alternatives of his own. He swapped senior commanders around, remonstrated with them and even made fun of them, sweetly assuring them at the same time that he was only an amateur, and would not dream of overruling their professional judgements. He wavered often, contradicting his own orders, and abruptly got rid of unsatisfactory commanders he had himself appointed: few top-ranking Union generals at the start of the war were still there at the end of it. In short he was one of the prime examples in the history of war of a meddling politician. Churchill thought – and he should know! – that Lincoln offered 'a classic instance of the dangers of civilian interference with generals in the field'. If the North had lost the conflict he would never have been forgiven.

The North won, though, and Lincoln has increasingly been recognized as a more remarkable strategist than most of his generals. He was a visionary amateur, in many ways foreseeing the manner of wars to come in the twentieth century – total wars, wars involving entire nations. He believed in attritional fighting, too, knowing that the far more populous North could afford to lose more soldiers than the South: the Union's priority should be destroying enemy armies rather than capturing enemy territory – the enemy soldiers might be their own people, but the purpose should be to kill as many of them as possible. Perhaps he remembered the fights of his youth in New Salem, of which it was said that their only rules were 'strike, gouge, bite, kick, anyway to win'. Could a war be fought, he once demanded of a squeamish critic, 'with elder-stalk squirts, charged with rose water?'

In minor military matters, personal matters, he was famously merciful. Time and again he reprieved soldiers sentenced to death for cowardice, or for falling asleep on sentry duty (it would frighten them too terribly, he once said, to have them shot). When the decrepit seventy-eight-year-old Brigadier-General John Wool found himself involved in disputes of rank, Lincoln was quite prepared to promote him to Major-General, if it would save hurting his feelings. In the wider conduct of the war, though, he was as ruthless as he was in politics. He admired the unforgiving hammer-blow, the annihilating battle, living off the country, no-holds-barred and surrender only on the victor's terms. When the most savagely brilliant of his generals, William Sherman, undertook his devastating march through Georgia, ravaging everything along the way and plunging the whole State into misery, Lincoln observed with satisfaction that the campaign had 'brought them that sit in darkness to see a great light'. When the milder General George Meade inflicted a decisive defeat upon the Confederates at Gettysburg, leaving them to limp away mangled and disheartened, Lincoln blamed him for not chasing and destroying them. He rejected more than one peace proposal in the course of the war: as the only acceptable price of settlement, he demanded the unconditional return of the secessionist States to the authority of the Union. The happiest moments of his Presidency were the moments of military success. After the Confederates were thwarted in an attempt to capture Philadelphia, Lincoln wrote a joyous piece of doggerel, putting it into the mouth of a bucolic Robert E. Lee:

> *In Eighteen sixty-three, with pomp, and mighty swell*
> *Me and Jeff's Confederacy, went forth to sack Phil-del,*
> *The Yankees they got arter us and giv us particular hell,*
> *And we skedadeled back again, and didn't sack Phil-del.*

In the course of the war he was served by a very mixed bag of generals. Many of the best senior officers, most of them trained at West Point, opted for the Southern side when the war began; among them was Lee himself, who was offered the command of the Union armies, but preferred to serve his home State of Virginia, and became the most admired American soldier of them all. The new senior officers Lincoln appointed were all too often political choices: Democratic officers, to keep the support of the Democratic party, foreign-born officers, to satisfy ethnic minorities, officers to assure the loyalties of regions, States or political constituencies. Some were incompetents, some even cowards – 'I who am not a specially brave man,' Lincoln once remarked, 'have had to sustain the sinking courage of these professional fighters.'

In the beginning Lincoln's chief commanders were Winfield Scott, seventy-four years old and so gouty as to be almost immobile, and George McClellan, dilatory and so conceited that he was nicknamed the Young Napoleon. By the end of his term he had found the inexorable Sherman, the diminutive and astute young cavalryman Philip Sheridan, and best of all Ulysses Simpson Grant, Lincoln's final General of the Army and a man after his own heart. In the months between he ran through a succession of commanders mostly forgotten to history, at least in Europe: Henry Halleck, W. S. Rosencrans, Benjamin Butler, Ambrose Burnside, John Pope, Irwin McDowell, George Meade, John C. Frémont, Don Carlos Buell, Joseph Hooker of Hooker's Division (whose own headquarters was once described as 'a combination of barroom and brothel').

With all these men Lincoln was frank and generally patient, sometimes even avuncular, if not always complimentary. His general view was that since the North had the greater numbers but the South the better communications, the Union forces should habitually threaten several different places at the same time, always being sure to attack the weaker ones. This ran counter to the accepted wisdom that forces ought to be concentrated for a single offensive, not scattered for several, and it seemed hard for his generals to grasp. Some of Lincoln's most pithy and cogent observations were made to (or about) his commanders. When a bombastic general crowed that it was not a question of *if* he would take Richmond, but *when*, Lincoln reminded him that the hen was the wisest of the animal creation, because she never cackled until the egg was laid. When the lines of a Southern army were particularly extended, he wired that 'the animal must be very slim somewhere. Could you not break him?' Rosencrans after a reverse was described as 'confused and stunned like a duck hit on the head'. Halleck in defeat was 'little more . . . than a first-rate clerk'. The slow-moving McClellan, an engineer by speciality, was said to have 'a special talent for the stationary engine'.

Lincoln's gift for graphic simplification served him well during these exchanges. A failed advance reminded him of an old woman trying to shoo her geese across a creek. A botched river-crossing was like having an ox with its front legs over one side of a fence and its back legs over the other. Grant once reported to him that Sherman, advancing southward across Georgia, 'might possibly be prevented from reaching the point he had started out to reach, but he would get through somewhere and would finally get to his chosen destination; and even if the worst came to the worst he could return North'. Lincoln interpreted this dispatch thus: 'If they cannot get out where they want to, they can crawl back by the hole they went in at.' To explain his strategy of being ready to attack all along an enemy line, rather than at points of concentration, he said it meant that troops who were not actually in action would be helping those who were – 'those not skinning could hold a leg'. Commenting on some fruitless attack upon an enemy strong-point, he observed that when he was a boy, if they came across a log in a field they used to plough round it; and this was perhaps consciously echoed forty years later by an American observer with the British Army in the Boer War, when he asked a battalion commander during a particularly ponderous and bloody assault upon a Boer-held hill, 'Say, colonel, isn't there a way *round*?'

The most difficult of all his generals was McClellan, who was to become his Democratic opponent in the Presidential campaign of 1864. This able, arrogant and flamboyant West Pointer, the son of a Philadelphia doctor, was a great trainer of armies, much admired by his soldiers, but he was temperamentally alien to Lincoln. The two men had known each other for years – during a hiatus in his military service McClellan had been chief engineer of the Illinois Central Railroad, and had arranged for Steven Douglas's special train in the 1858 debates. They had never much liked each other. The most McClellan would say of Lincoln as a Chief Executive was that he was 'a rare bird'. Later he liked to call him 'the original Gorilla', and when Lincoln and his Secretary of State once called on him in his house in Washington he went to bed without bothering to see them. He used to say that he couldn't tell Lincoln all his plans because the President would pass them on to Tad, and the next morning they would be in the New York *Herald* – a gibe simultaneously at Lincoln's passion for his little boy, and at Mary Lincoln's unsuitable acquaintances. 'I can never regard him with feelings other than those of thorough contempt' – but he bombarded his Commander-in-Chief nevertheless with rambling petulant letters and telegrams of complaint.

For his part Lincoln was exasperated by McClellan's caution in the field, especially in launching offensives. He preferred more gung-ho generals. 'McClellan has the slows,' he would complain, as though it were a digestive disorder, but at other times he wondered if there was a touch of treason there. He thought McClellan consistently overstated the size of the forces opposing him, as an excuse for failing to move, and grumbled too much about lack of resources and supplies, about inadequate support from Washington, about exhausted men and fatigued horses. 'Will you pardon me for asking,' Lincoln once wired, 'what the horses of your army have done since the battle of Antietam that fatigue anything?' He said that if General McClellan did not want to use the army, he would like to borrow it himself, and in his dealings with the Young Napoleon Lincoln certainly lived up to Churchill's characterization of him as an interfering civilian. At one time or another messages from the White House urged the unfortunate general to act, to stand firm, to have none of it, to hold firm as with a chain of steel, to force it, or to yield only inch by inch and in good order – very like Churchill himself in 1942 ordering the hapless imperial armies of Singapore to fight to the last man. When the Emancipation Proclamation was published McClellan declared it 'infamous in the extreme', and told his wife that he could not 'fight for such a cursed doctrine as that of a servile insurrection' – so perhaps there really was a tinge of disloyalty to his actions all along. He was relieved of his command in 1862, was easily beaten by the Original Gorilla in their Presidential contest, and in the tradition of Hilaire Belloc's unsuccessful Lord Lundy – 'Go out and govern New South Wales!' – wound up as Governor of New Jersey.

Very different were Lincoln's relations with Ulysses S. Grant, the West Point graduate who became General-in-Chief in 1864. Grant had never met the President before then, but had fought so successfully during the past years that he was received at the White House like a conquering hero. He was just Lincoln's man. He smoked too many cigars, he drank a lot of whiskey, he had left the army in 1854 to become a clerk in a leather-goods store in Illinois, but he was a fighter through and through, as willing as the President himself to hurl his forces into battle come what may. He was also, so Lincoln observed with approval, 'a very meagre writer or telegrapher'. There was no need to interfere with Grant. 'The particulars of your plans,' the President once wired him, 'I neither know or seek to know.' 'I begin to see it,' he telegraphed as one of Grant's offensives unfolded, 'you will succeed,' and he was merely agreeing, not adjuring, when he said that Grant should 'hold on with a bulldog grip, and chew & choke, as much as possible'. The partnership was a triumphant success; four years after their victory Grant himself became the eighteenth President of the United States.

And how would Lincoln have got on, I wonder, with his charismatic equivalent on the other side of the line, Robert E. Lee, General-in-Chief of the Confederate Army? They were the twin champions of the war, legendary in their own lifetimes and beloved of their respective armies – 'No, no, don't go any further, General,' Lee's soldiers cried when he got too close to the enemy lines – 'Get down, you damned fool!' shouted the young captain when Lincoln stood on the rampart at Fort Stevens. They never met, but we can imagine they did. Picture Robert E. Lee, the very model of a Southern patrician, heroic son of 'Light Horse Harry' Lee, awaiting the arrival of Abraham Lincoln at some neutral meeting-place. There he stands, a little under six feet tall, with delicate feet meticulously shod, gracefully posed before the fireplace in his impeccable uniform – sash around his waist, sword at his side, on his face an expression of perfect gentlemanliness. His eyes are brown and generous, his hair is elegantly grey above a noble brow, his beard is beautifully groomed. Even at West Point his fellow cadets had called him the 'Marble Model', and one of them had noted his 'beautifully symmetrical' limbs, and said his step was 'as elastic as if he spurned the ground he trod on'.

I don't think I would have much taken to this paragon of Southern chivalry, *sans peur et sans reproche*, and it would be a relief for me when Lincoln stumped in, 'as if he needed oiling', with his clothes that didn't fit him very well, his huge feet and Tad hanging on to his hand. 'Why, General, this meeting of ours reminds me of the story of the old woman and the doctor at the county fair – do you happen to know that tale, Sir? It was like this . . .' Lee would, I have no doubt, courteously have laughed at the anecdote, but not half so much as Tad and Lincoln would, or even me.

The civil war was fought on two major land fronts, and at sea. At sea the Union navy maintained an unrelenting blockade of all the Southern ports, aiming to ruin the cotton trade which was the economic engine of the Confederacy. In the west Union strategy falteringly resolved itself into campaigns to gain control of the Mississippi River. In the east the tasks of the Army of the Potomac, the most powerful of the Union armies, were to protect the North from invasion, destroy Lee's forces, and eventually capture the Confederate capital of Richmond. Lincoln never visited the western fighting fronts, but he kept close links with his forces nearer home.

Eleven times during his Presidency he visited them, to stimulate his generals into more resolute action, but also to keep in touch with the common soldiers, and experience some of war's hardships and excitements for himself. His appearance generally amused the soldiery at first. One young officer described him as the ugliest man he ever saw – 'like a highly intelligent satyr'. Others were entertained by his country horsemanship: often the horse he was given was too small for him, his toes almost seemed to touch the ground and barrack-room wags said the best thing to do would be to tie his legs together under the animal's belly. Sometimes his hat looked as though it was going to fall off, and once at least it was knocked off by the branch of a tree. Most comical of all, his trousers had a habit of creeping up as he rode, until his white long johns showed.

Sometimes the men could not help laughing, but the President always responded to their ribaldry with kind dignity, laughing, too, and removing his hat in salute. He had the power to touch them, and they very soon subsided first into a respectful silence, and then into profound applause. If the President was inspecting them, no less were they inspecting the President, and hundreds of them wrote home about the experience. His face looked so tired and sad, they nearly all said, and I suppose at heart they knew him for what he was, not just another meretricious politician or posturing visiting brass-hat, still less some sort of clown, but the most formidable of all their leaders, with the mightiest responsibilities. 'There must be a heap of trouble on the old man's mind,' one soldier wrote. 'Abraham looks poorly,' wrote another. 'I could but pity as I looked at him, and remembered the weight of responsibility resting upon his burdened mind.' When they cheered him, they did so with sympathy. 'The men could not be restrained from so honouring him,' wrote Private Rice Bull of New York. 'He really was the ideal of the Army.'

Prisoners from the other side, too, when a shipload of them saw Lincoln passing one day down the Potomac River, ran to the rails to cheer him. Neither his own men nor the enemy, perhaps, realized how lethal a strategist their Father Abraham was.

For years one epicentre of conflict was the stretch of water called the Hampton Roads, where the James River runs into Chesapeake Bay and the Atlantic. This is one of the great natural harbours of the world, and is a terrific spectacle always. It looks rather like a lake. The wide James flows in from the west, away to the east there is a suggestion of the open Atlantic. On the southern shore stands Norfolk, Virginia, the principal naval base of the world, and on the city's flank, among the derricks and chimneys of its shipyards, there stand always the mighty superstructures of aircraft carriers, with cruisers and destroyers berthed alongside them, and radar towers above. On the northern side of the Roads a great Stars and Stripes flies above the ramparts of Fort Monroe, built to protect them from sea attack; on the skyline beyond is Chesapeake Bay Bridge, a prodigious road-and-tunnel work which links Norfolk with the upper eastern shore of Virginia, and one can just make out the glint of cars and trucks streaming across it. And always there are ships in sight: hulking container ships labouring down from Baltimore, sleek grey Aegis cruisers sweeping towards their berths, white fishing craft tossing in the swell, or most unforgettable of all one of those stupendous carriers, *Nimitz* or *Washington* or even USS *Abraham Lincoln*, more like a floating castle than a ship, magnificently passing Fort Monroe to take its aircraft and its missiles to some distant foreign trouble-spot – for nowadays it is out of the Hampton Roads, more than anywhere, that the long arm of American power reaches across the oceans.

The place was hardly less significant in Lincoln's day. It was the obvious base for naval operations all along the eastern seaboard, and it also provided access, by way of the navigable river system, to Richmond at the heart of the Confederacy. During the first part of his Presidency Norfolk and all the southern shore of the Roads were in Confederate hands, but the Union held Fort Monroe and the northern shore, and here there was fought a seminal battle between two revolutionary warships, CSS (Confederate States Ship) *Virginia* and USS *Monitor*. The *Virginia* was an ironclad, built upon the hull of a wooden steam frigate, the *Merrimac*, which had been abandoned at Norfolk by the Union navy. She was a slab-sided armoured ship, like a floating metal box, ponderous, slow and high in the water, with two funnels and a battery of ten mixed-calibre guns. In the spring of 1862 she emerged terrifyingly out of nowhere to wreak havoc among Federal vessels in the Roads, but almost at once there appeared from the north the *Monitor*, an even more radical fighting ship. Just as heavily armoured, she was in some ways the opposite of *Virginia*, extremely low in the water, more manœuvrable and armed with two 11-inch guns in a revolving turret. The behemoths met and slugged it out in a battle that made all wooden warships obsolescent at a stroke, but resulted in a draw, neither ship being able to penetrate the other's iron plate. The *Monitor* withdrew to lick her wounds. The *Virginia* was left to hang around Norfolk presenting a constant fearful threat to the Union – like a rocket missile of the day, which might (it was thought) at any time appear on the Potomac to bombard Washington, or even sail up the ocean coast to New York.

In the Northern imagination the *Virginia* became the kind of monster mothers evoked to scare recalcitrant children, and to Washington strategists she was one of the heaviest factors in the balance of the war. No conventional warship could stand up to her fire, and her mere existence inhibited Union campaigning in the east. She was a one-ship fleet-in-being – all alone she was stalemating the war. 'This man Rommel is a nuisance,' Montgomery had told his troops before the Battle of Alamein, and Lincoln felt rather the same about the *Virginia*. He reached the conclusion that the only sure way of dealing with her was to capture Norfolk, the ironclad's base, and in May 1862 he decided to go to Fort Monroe to arrange the matter for himself (i.e., 'to ascertain by personal observation whether some further vigilance and vigor might not be infused into the operations').

This was an exhilarating initiative. Taking Chase and

Stanton with him, the President sailed down to Hampton
Roads, by way of the Potomac and Chesapeake Bay,
on board the spanking *Miami*, a brand-new sidewheel
gunboat which the Treasury used as a revenue cutter.
At Fort Monroe he put up at an elegant house called
No. 1 The Ramparts, which still stands most welcomingly
inside the fort's main gates, and looks less like an American
army quarter than a Governor's residence within some
imperial fortress of the Indies. He inspected the garrison
of course, and accepted a twenty-one-gun salute, and
saw the great 15-inch cannon which was named for him,
and in such stylish circumstances he personally planned
the taking of Norfolk – his most direct and decisive
intervention in the running of the war. The President
of the United States and his Secretary of War actually
took a boat over to the enemy shore, to reconnoitre the
best place for a landing, and Lincoln insisted on taking
a moonlight walk along the beach. He was eagerly watching, too, when six of his ships opened a bombardment
of the Norfolk dockyards, and a Union assault force
assembled for embarkation.

Hardly had the soldiers started to board their transports
when there slid out of Sleeman Creek, close to where
the carriers lie today, the ominous towering shape of
Virginia herself. It was Lincoln's first and only sight
of the ship, so literally his *bête noire*, and I can easily
envisage its almost hallucinatory appearance now, when
I stand myself on the foreshore of Fort Monroe: dark,
and slow, and clumsy, and awful. The operation was
temporarily called off – an amphibious force in the Roads
would be mincemeat for *Virginia*'s guns: but two days

later, when the monster was back skulking in its lair, the crossing was safely made and Norfolk was captured.

Even as the Union troops marched into the city, accompanied by the Secretary of the Treasury, a great black cloud arose over Sleeman Creek – the legendary ironclad was being blown up by its crew. Lincoln returned to Washington in high spirits, his mission accomplished. 'So ended,' wrote Chase, not always among Lincoln's greatest admirers, 'a brilliant week's campaigning of the President . . . If he had not come down . . . the [*Virginia* would have been] as grim and defiant and as much a terror as ever.'

More than once Lincoln visited his generals directing campaigns against Richmond – or more often bogged down in their laborious advances towards the enemy capital. These visits had a symbolical flavour, because commanders habitually requisitioned, as commanders will, the most splendid houses in their occupied territory; and some of the most splendid houses in all America were the plantation mansions that stood in elegant enfilade along the banks of the James River, the waterway leading to Richmond. They represented the ultimate in Southern civilization. They were Robert E. Lee in masonry! With their stately colonnaded porticos, their lavish outbuildings and their glorious acres of cotton or tobacco, generally looking through holm oaks and beeches to the river gently flowing below, they were enough to test the resolution of an abolitionist – for they were, of course, one and all founded upon the Peculiar Institution.

What did the slaves think, I wonder, when the future Great Emancipator arrived in his carriage, with his mounted bodyguard, at such a house as Berkeley at Harrison's Landing, where General McClellan set up his headquarters in 1862 surrounded by an encampment of 140,000 soldiers? Berkeley, whose publicists now like to call it 'the Most Historic Plantation in Virginia', had undoubtedly imprinted its glory upon the minds of its least imaginative or dissatisfied blacks. It was a fine Georgian red-brick house, all symmetrical urbanity, partly simple, partly grand, with acres of terraced pleasure gardens leading to the river in an epitome of Virginian grace and hospitality. The very first Thanksgiving service had been held there, on the river bank in 1619. The very first American bourbon was distilled there, in 1621, and a white domed gazebo above the river was specifically dedicated to the serving of mint juleps. Benjamin Harrison IV, whose father built the house, was a signatory of the Declaration of Independence. George Washington and the next seven Presidents all visited Berkeley; the ninth, William Harrison, was born in the house, and his grandson Benjamin Harrison became the twenty-third. It was the grandest of the grand mansions along the James, the focus of the planters' social life; and doubtless the slaves of the estate, acclimatized to such lofty assurance, like the servants of patricians around the world regarded it all with semi-proprietorial pride.

Well, here comes the army of the Yankees, to mess up the property with its huts and wagons and parade grounds, and its tents all over the wide lawns. Here comes Massa McClellan, the new overseer of Berkeley, a proud little man indeed with his gold stripes and his epaulettes, his droopy moustache and the little black beard on his chin, but hardly a Virginia aristocrat. And now here comes Ol' Man Lincoln himself, the bogyman of the South, and law sakes, what a funny looking sight *he* is. A hundred thousand soldiers parade on the upper meadow to salute him, and here he comes in his black suit like a minister, and his high hat, all gawky, as though he doesn't know to put one foot in front of the other – bless my soul, you can't help laughing. Get away now, Bessie, that old nigger John says, quit that laughing, that's the gentleman that's going to make a lady of you – but bless you, he ain't like no gentleman at all, not like the late Mr Harrison, God bless his soul, or Mr Robert E. Lee, a proper gentleman if ever there was one. I did see that Mr Robert E. Lee with my own eyes, when he came down here from Shirley up the river, and if I was to put my cent on one of those gentleman or the other, why it'd go on Mr Robert E. Lee every time . . .

And how did President Lincoln respond to Berkeley? Perhaps his mind went back to those comforting times with Josh Speed at Farmington, and Morocco the coachman, and wandering through the scented gardens in the evening, when just for a moment he had allowed himself to fancy living life as a Southern planter: and I dare say he marvelled, as he noticed Bessie stifling her giggles, that here he was the master of the Most Historic Plantation in Virginia, more powerful than any Harrison, a hundred thousand men mustered to salute him and the fate of every slave in America in his hands.

★

The fighting was over at Gettysburg, Pennsylvania, when Lincoln arrived for a night and a day in November 1863, but the men killed in battle there four months before had not yet been properly buried, and rain was starting to uncover their shallow graves. It had been the most fateful battle of the entire conflict. At this small market-town, 75 miles from Washington, the armies had met more or less by chance and slaughtered some 46,000 of each other – attritional war with a vengeance. Robert E. Lee had advanced a hill too far into Pennsylvania; his second-in-command George Pickett failed in an heroic charge upon the Union lines; the Union could afford to lose 20,000 men, the Confederacy could not. Although the war was to continue for another two years, at Gettysburg the eventual defeat of the Confederacy was clinched. Lincoln's visit was not celebratory, though. He came, by train from Washington, not to congratulate his victorious troops, but to speak at the dedication ceremony for a new cemetery, within sight of the battlefield, in which the Union dead were to be permanently buried.

In retrospect now it was a stroke of fortune for Gettysburg that the armies chanced to fight the most tragic of all their battles on the edge of town, and a greater bit of luck still when Lincoln agreed to speak at the cemetery. The town has never looked back, and has long left all rivals behind as the most famous country community in America. It is a cross between Lourdes and Waterloo. It lives partly by its possession of the killing grounds in the meadows all around, and partly by Lincoln's speech at the cemetery, perhaps the best-known declamation in all the annals of oratory. Nowadays you would hardly know it had ever been a plain Pennsylvania rural community. In the battlefield itself, which half-surrounds the town, hundreds of separate monuments sustain the memory of the carnage, and are haunted by platoons of schoolchildren wearing bits of uniform and carrying flags, and by indefatigable bearded buffs retracing ancient skirmishes among the shrubbery. A man I once met inspecting antique buttons in a Gettysburg Militaria shop needed them to complete his equipment for next day's reenactment of Pickett's Charge, in which every strap, buckle and button must be authentic.

Not for a moment can one forget Lincoln's visit to the town. Here is the house where he finished writing his speech, the night before he delivered it. Here is a statue of him in Lincoln Square, and a bust of him around the corner. When I once stepped into Abe's Antiques to buy a video of D. W. Griffith's *Abraham Lincoln* I was not in the least surprised to find myself served by an extremely convincing Lincoln look-alike. And the spot where Lincoln delivered his address is a very shrine of Lincoln shrines. The memorial near by is said to be the only monument in America to a speech rather than a speaker, and the full address is reproduced there in bronze upon a plaque, with Lincoln's signature at the end of it. The wooded hills of Pennsylvania stand all around, the cemetery is rich in grand old trees, pilgrims for ever wander reverently among the lawns, and sceptic that I am I found myself almost superstitiously moved by the numen of the place. When I turned to go I noticed that the sun had caught a single word on the plaque which had evidently been rubbed shiny by the touch of

a million forefingers – like Lincoln's luminous nose at
his tomb in Springfield. I went back to see what word
it was, and found it was the pronoun 'We', as in 'We
the People.'

A far less sombre occasion was Lincoln's visit in March
1865 to City Point, on the right bank of the James River
some 50 miles below Richmond. Now the war was
almost won, and Ulysses S. Grant was the Union General-
in-Chief. He was preparing a last assault upon Richmond,
which had long been under siege, and had set up his
headquarters at another plantation house, Appomattox
Manor, among fields of cotton on a high bluff above
the river. This was a more workmanlike set-up than
McClellan's Berkeley three years before, and already had
a powerful air of success to it. It looked astonishing. The
military engineers had built a railway line to link City
Point with the front line 8 miles away, and 26 locomotives
hauled 275 boxcars backwards and forwards, night and
day, to supply the armies poised for a final advance. Nine
million soldiers' meals, 12,000 tons of fodder and 100,000
bread rations were routinely stockpiled at City Point.
The little river-landing below the Appomattox bluff had
been transformed into one of the busiest river ports in
the world, a constant terrific bustle of steamboats, sailing
ships, barges, skiffs and dinghies, jammed together off
shore in a babel of shouts, clankings and hammerings.
Clouds of steam and smoke habitually hung over the
landing, and the trains came and went, the ships dropped
their anchors or warped their way into the river, the
trains of horse-wagons rumbled by, as in some great

industrial port – Liverpool, say. City Point was a revelation of modern warfare.

Lincoln came from Washington, at Grant's invitation, in confident and buoyant mood, with Mary and Tad to keep him company. The war was ending! He had sailed down the Potomac into Chesapeake Bay, then through the Roads and up the James in the steamer *River Queen*, a graceful stern-wheeler with a high white superstructure and twin funnels which served him as a Presidential yacht. Appomattox was nothing like as grand as Berkeley, which was just in sight through binoculars across the water, and by now was almost swamped by the military. In the pleasant house itself (so its unhappy owner later complained) windows were smashed, furniture was broken and graffiti covered the walls. On the estate trees had been cut down and fences destroyed, and the whole of the high ground above the river was crowded with huts and with the tents of a military hospital. None of this shows now. Today City Point is part of Hopewell, Virginia, and is a National Historic District. All is calm and serene again, the trees are replanted and the house has been restored by the National Park Service. Only the green fields by the river are still stamped flat by the feet of dockers long ago, and rutted by the wheels of a thousand wagons; and sometimes a river tug ties up in the shade of the trees, and its crew sun themselves on deck, smoking.

Lincoln stayed at City Point for a fortnight, sleeping on board the *River Queen*, and driving each day up a winding track for his meetings with the General-in-Chief on the bluff above. It was characteristic of Grant that he did not have quarters in the manor house at all, but lived and worked in a wooden cabin among the dozen huts of his headquarters. He was no Young Napoleon, no Marble Model either. He looked rather like a Scottish terrier, a short, broad, blunt man with a bristly, stubbly beard and sharp eyes. He slouched. He usually dressed as a private soldier, except for the stars of rank upon his shoulder, and he was methodical, implacable and if I am to go by his memoirs rather humourless. He was a devoted family man, and his wife and six-year-old son Jesse were living in the cabin too, but still I fear it smelt of cigar smoke and whiskey ('Grant's Particular,' the President called it, and he said that if it would make all his generals fight as well, he would send them a barrel each).

It was meant to be a holiday for the Lincolns, and a healthy change of air for Abraham. Mary was looked after by Mrs Grant (with insufficient respect, she thought); Tad spent much of the time messing about on the *River Queen* and some of it, I hope, playing with Jesse. Lincoln himself was certainly not idle. He visited front-line troops, he was introduced to generals, he shook the hands, it was claimed, of 6,000 men in the hospital tents, he inspected the usual parades and befriended a couple of motherless kittens (*'Colonel! Get them some milk, and don't let them starve!'*). And incessantly he discussed with Grant the final offensive then developing. They went together to the HQ signals office to follow the news from the battle-front. They pored over maps at the general's desk. They looked down from the ravaged cotton fields at the stupen-dous spectacle of the quays below, and the supplies flowing endlessly ashore. One day General Sherman paid a lightning visit to talk about his part in the coming push. Couldn't they avoid another bloody battle? Lincoln asked, but Sherman said it wasn't up to them, it was up to the enemy. With victory in sight at last, though, Lincoln was in conciliatory mood, and he was already thinking about how to treat the defeated enemy: 'Let them surrender and go home, they won't take up arms again. Let them all go, officers and all, let them have their horses to plow with, and, if you like, their guns to shoot crows with.'

Five days later, on 3 April 1865, Richmond fell.

And it was to Richmond, the very next morning, that President Lincoln made his last operational foray. Never mind that the city was presumably full of embittered and hostile Southerners, or that Lee's retreating troops had set fire to its tobacco warehouses, leaving acres in ruins. Never mind that Stanton had respectfully telegraphed asking if the President really ought to 'expose the nation to the consequence of any disaster to yourself'. Richmond, the capital of the rebel Confederacy, had fallen; to Richmond the President of the United States must go; to Richmond, taking Tad with him, he went. An odd little fleet took him upstream from City Point, accompanied by Admiral David Porter, his naval commander, by a personal bodyguard, William D. Crook, by a troop of cavalry and by twelve stalwart marines, for safety's sake. First went a tug, *Glance*, towing a barge with the marines on board; then the graceful *River Queen*; then the *Malvern*, a captured Confederate gun-runner which was Admiral Porter's flagship; and finally the transport *Columbus* bringing the cavalry escort. Grant telegraphed his commander in the captured city, General Godfrey Weitzel, to warn him the President was on his way.

The convoy didn't get far, though. Upriver the channel proved to be blocked with debris, and none of the bigger ships could get through. The President and his companions were transferred into *Glance*'s barge, along with the marines, but the tug went aground, the tow was cut and they had to be rowed. The cavalry were left behind. Lincoln said it reminded him of a man who, having been turned down for a ministerial appointment somewhere, asked to be made a customs officer instead and finally settled for a pair of trousers – '*but it is well to be humble!*' At last they entered the purlieus of Richmond, but their arrival was hardly less bathetic. When they reached the steamboat wharf at Rocketts Landing they found no welcoming troops or carriage from General Weitzel's command, only a crowd of inquisitive blacks. What to do? Lincoln, the Admiral, Captain John Barnes of the *Malvern*, Crook, the marines, Tad and all conferred, and finally it was decided that the President of the United States must walk the two miles into the centre of the conquered capital. He took his topcoat off. It was no triumphal entry, but it was one of Lincoln's great moments all the same.

Black clouds of smoke still hung over Richmond, and smuts blew about the air in the slummy quarters down by the landing-place. Resolutely Lincoln strode along the rough road towards the city centre, holding Tad by the hand, with Porter, Barnes and Crook following dubiously, and the marines (I think we may assume) nervously clutching their carbines. No Union troops appeared to greet them. They walked on through fast-assembling crowds, between blackened ruins, towards the government buildings on a hill in the heart of the place. Everything looked shabby, everyone looked half-starved, the streets were full of rubbish and broken glass, and there was certainly no welcome from the white citizens. They mostly watched in silence from the side-walks; on the steps of grand houses a few women stood haughty and immobile. On the other hand among the Negroes, who knew that for better or for worse a Union victory meant freedom for themselves, a frenzied rejoic-ing stirred. Soon black men and women were throwing themselves with theatrical fervour before the President, jostling around him and shouting, 'Father Abraham! Abraham Lincum! Glory, glory! Hallelujah!' A woman cried, 'I know I'm free, 'cos I've seen Father Abraham, and felt him.' One old man fell at the President's feet, until Lincoln gently told him to get up – 'don't kneel to me, that's not right, you must kneel to God only.' Another, tears running down his cheeks, removed his hat and said: 'May the good Lord bless you, President Linkum.' Lincoln lifted his own hat and bowed in return – 'a death shock for the chivalry', wrote a watching reporter.

They found General Weitzel at last, and he put at their disposal an army hack, drawn by four horses. In it Lincoln and Tad made a tour of the city, Crook riding horseback beside them. Past Robert E. Lee's house they went (inside was Mrs Lee, laid low by arthritis), and past the house of General Pickett, of Pickett's Charge at Gettysburg (whose wife, she herself later claimed, came to the door to receive some kind words from the President), and they stopped at the State House of Virginia, which had also been for four years the Capitol of the Confederacy. Capitol Square in Richmond is one of the great architectural ensembles of America. Around its green expanse are the offices of Government, the Governor's House and a heroic equestrian statue of George Washington: in the middle, high above the city like the Parthenon above Athens, stands the Capitol, designed by Thomas Jefferson himself. Today the building has been weakened rather by the addition of wings: when Lincoln saw it that day, for the first time in his life, it was just as Jefferson intended it, a grand paean to the ideals of the classical age and the American Revolution. Its model was La Maison Carrée at Nîmes, which Jefferson considered the noblest of all the structures of antiquity, and it stood there alone on its high plinth, proud and magnificent, looking over the city to the river far below.

By the time I got to Capitol Square in 1998, and turned to survey that prospect, before me was a lively townscape of skyscrapers, offices and motorways, with fine modern bridges crossing the rocky James to the south. When Lincoln looked in the same direction, all he saw was desolation – streets of gaunt burnt-out buildings, pot-holed roadways littered with wreckage, and three shattered bridges over the river, blown up by Lee's retreating army. Downstream, on the opposite bank, the Confederate Navy Yard was a mess of wrecked machinery and scuttled gunboats. Belle Isle in mid-stream, used as a prisoner-of-war camp by the Confederates, was covered with dingy huts. Forlorn to the east were the 150 single-storey buildings of Chimborazo, said to be the biggest military hospital on earth, where 75,000 wounded soldiers had been treated in the course of the war, and thousands still lay. Capitol Square itself was crowded with refugees, and littered with their poor piles of possessions: around its edges Union infantry had pitched their tents and stacked their rifles, and cavalrymen had hitched their horses to the railings. Richmond in April 1865 was a miserable image of defeat, and perhaps Lincoln felt some tremor of embarrassment in riding through it like Tamerlane through Persepolis, if only in a borrowed carriage with Tad.

They pulled up at the main entrance of the Capitol, and Lincoln went inside. The Confederate Legislature was dispersed, Jefferson Davis had fled to the South, and the great building was empty. What did he do? I asked the kind ladies at the Capitol information desk, when I was there myself. They seemed uncertain. 'He went in there,' they decided, pointing to the old Senate chamber, so I went in there myself. The most prominent thing in the room now is a statue of General Lee, and although it was certainly not there when Lincoln walked in that day, the name and image of Robert E. Lee must have crossed his mind all the same. It was in this chamber, four years before, that Lee had accepted the House's invitation to command the armies of the Confederacy: it surely occurred to Lincoln then that if Lee had instead accepted the invitation to command the armies of the Union, he and Tad might have been in Richmond long before . . .

'Mr Lincoln didn't stay in this building long,' the ladies told me, and I knew that to be true. He had been more interested in visiting the Confederate White House, Davis's Executive Mansion, which is a grand classical building almost adjacent to the Capitol. I knew just what he did there, too, because it is recorded in a dozen diaries. He went upstairs to Jefferson Davis's office, and there he seated himself in Davis's own Presidential chair. For a few moments, we are told, he was lost in thought. Four years of bitter trial, we may fancy, passed through his tired mind then: defeats and victories, quarrels and friendships, cruel cartoons and sycophantic addresses, that torrent of visitors pouring through his own White House, Mary and her drapery bills, little Willie leaving them, Tom Thumb and Hole in the Day and the one-legged beggar, infuriating McClellan and fat old Winfield Scott, *Virginia* creeping out of Sleeman Cove, nights of exhaustion by the telegraph machine, the cadences of his own prose, the cheers and catcalls of the fickle crowd. It was almost over now. In a few weeks Grant would put an end to it all. Abe Lincoln eased himself from Jefferson Davis's chair, picked up his hat, shook hands with General Weitzel and returned to Rocketts Landing.

During the voyage home to Washington he entertained his companions by reading Shakespeare to them: in particular, twice over, *Macbeth* Act III, Scene 2, lines 22ff.:

> *Duncan is in his grave;*
> *After life's fitful fever he sleeps well;*
> *Treason has done his worst: nor steel, nor poison,*
> *Malice domestic, foreign levy, nothing*
> *Can touch him further.*

Six

The artist — use of language — a voice of his own — into the sublime — becoming America — his life an art form — betrayal, premonition and the empty tracks

For me the coming of the absolute Lincoln was signalled by the farewell speech at Springfield which provides the transitional interlude of this book. It is the first thing he wrote that can touch my heart, and send a shiver down my spine. He was fifty-two then: four years later the challenges of war and statesmanship had finally moulded his personality, and he stood for all to see as one of nature's born aristocrats — not a gentleman exactly, as Aunt Bessie at Berkeley had perceived, but a native aristocrat. He must have realized by then that his innately patrician eccentricities, his natural disregard for petty matters of money and appearance, his indifference to bourgeois niceties of behaviour, represented his proper level in life. A middle-class lawyer could not appropriately go to his front door in shirtsleeves and flip-flop slippers, but a President could. A yeoman farmer from East Anglia might care if his trousers were too short or his cravat was loose, but a Welsh prince wouldn't.

Nor would a poet: for I have come to think that the celebrated enigmas of President Lincoln's character – 'inexplicable' and 'mysterious' as they were called in his own lifetime – were not enigmas at all, but the characteristics of an artist. The moods, the contradictions, the evasiveness, the questioning of accepted truths, the sexual complexity, the play-acting, the sad resolution and the power to move the spirit, all made a poet of this consummate politician. Perhaps he knew it all along. When he boarded that train at Springfield he surely realized that the curtain was about to go up on a majestic drama, more Shakespearian than anything in Weems' *Life and Memorable Actions of George Washington*. When he looked across the ruins of Richmond the victorious conclusion of the war – *his* war – must have seemed to him like the tragic coda of a symphony (except that, so far as I know, he never heard a symphony in his life).

He was never a truly cultivated man. He seems to have had no visual interests, and my guess is that he was red-green colour-blind, accounting for the mismatched socks he often wore. Mary said she failed to teach him the difference between pink and blue, and he never liked flowers much: 'I don't know why it's so,' he said, 'but I seem to have no taste, natural or acquired, for such things.' When he saw the Niagara Falls for the first time, he told Herndon, 'the thing that struck me most forcibly was, where in the world did all that water come from?' He couldn't sing a line, either, and his musical preferences were for simple ballads, opera arias of the more vibrant kind and marches ('Dixie' was a favourite – the war song of the South, captured he liked to say in battle, although the tune was actually composed by a loyal Northerner, Daniel Decatur Emmett). He loved to hear Ward Lamon play Stephen Foster tunes on the banjo, and when he sponsored the first ever concert in the White House the performers included a midget from Barnum's Circus, who sang 'Columbia, the Gem of the Ocean', and an American Indian singer billed as 'the Aboriginal Jenny Lind'. He was fond of the theatre, but indiscriminately, almost as pleased by a performance of some thin farce as he was by *Hamlet* (and he was a bit of a ham actor himself for much of the time, varying his part according to his audience, in the politician's way).

Yet in the use of language he turned out to be a master. He had great tutors there: the translators of the King James Bible, the magic chroniclers of the Arabian Nights, Aesop of the Fables, Bunyan and Milton and Burns and Alexander Pope. Like most of us, he knew only parts of Shakespeare, but he knew them very well, and he liked reading them more than seeing them acted. He enjoyed the down–home satiric humour of American writers like Artemus Ward and Petroleum V. Nasby, and he stored up stories from the comic collections popular then. He was always fascinated by English grammar, though his spelling remained for ever unreliable. He loved antithesis and antiphony. Early in life he recognized the power of rhythm in prose.

Out of this mish-mash of artistic influences, banal to magnificent, Lincoln eventually distilled a literary style all his own. '*Le style est l'homme même*,' the Frenchman George-Louis de Buffon decreed, but Lincoln's did not come naturally to him. Most of his early writing and speaking was thoroughly derivative. His earliest known composition, written in a school exercise book when he was fourteen, sounds to me like one of those backyard jingles all schoolchildren know –

> *Abraham Lincoln*
> *His hand and pen*
> *He will be good but*
> *God knows when*

– on a par with the New Jersey favourite 'What's your name?/John Brown./Ask me again/And I'll knock you down.'

His early attempts at poetry are watered-down Gray's 'Elegy', his adolescent satirical verse is crudely copy-cat, and much of his oratory is embarrassingly fustian or overblown, in the idiom of the day. What could be much worse than this peroration to a speech of 1839 concerning a new kind of depository for government funds?

If ever I feel the soul within me elevate and expand to those dimensions not wholly unworthy of its Almighty Architect, it is when I contemplate the cause of my country, deserted by all the world beside, and I standing up boldly and alone and hurling defiance at her victorious oppressors. Here, without contemplating consequences, before High Heaven, and in the face of the world, I swear eternal fidelity to the just cause, as I deem it, of the land of my life, my liberty and my love.

And what about this extract from his eulogy in 1850 for President Zachary Taylor?

And now the din of battle nears the fort and sweeps obliquely by . . . they fly to the wall; every eye is strained – it is – it is – the stars and stripes are still aloft!

The Lincoln style could be downright trashy, as when he described the black soldiers of his army remembering that 'with silent tongue and clenched teeth and steady eye and well-poised bayonet they have helped mankind on to this great consummation.' Sometimes a cheaply patriotic, newsreel note was sounded:

The signs look better. The Father of Waters again goes un-vexed to the sea. Thanks to the great Northwest for it. Nor yet wholly to them. Three hundred miles up, they met New England, Empire, Keystone, and Jersey, hewing their way right and left. The Sunny South, too, in more colors than one, also lent a hand . . .

When religiosity crept in it made Lincoln's rhetoric feel more artificial still, as in his proclamation of Thanks-giving in 1863 (*'no human counsel hath devised, nor hath any mortal hand worked out these great things . . .'*), but even some of his most historic political addresses could be

florid enough. This for instance is the end of his famous
'House Divided' speech, at Springfield in 1858, when all
he was doing was urging his fellow Republicans to
emulate the party's successes in elections two years before:

Of strange, discordant and even hostile elements we gathered
from the four winds, and formed and fought the battle through,
under the constant hot fire of a disciplined, proud and pam-
pered enemy.

Did we brave all then to falter now? – now – when that
same enemy is wavering, dissevered, and belligerent?

The result is not doubtful. We shall not fail – if we stand
firm, we shall not fail.

I think Lincoln first found a voice of his own in his
homely wisecracks, retorts, puns and images. They were
not always his invention, but he gave them a particular
pith. An improbable assertion was 'as thin as the homeopathic soup that was made by boiling a shadow of a pigeon
that had been starved to death'. A specious argument was
like confusing a chestnut horse with a horse-chestnut. A
plethora of place-seekers looking for too few jobs was
'too many pigs for the tits'. An army officer accused of
being a Peeping Tom 'should be elevated to the peerage'.
Asked by a young woman in a hospital to tell her just
where in his body her boyfriend had been wounded –
he had refused to tell her himself – Lincoln blushed and
said: 'Ma'am, the bullet that wounded him wouldn't
have wounded you.' This is his description of the hunt
for a missing person, at Springfield in 1841:

Away the People swept like a herd of buffaloes, and cut down
Hickoxes mill dam *nolens volens*, to draw the water out of the
pond; and then went up and down, and down and up the
creek, fishing and raking, and ducking and diving for two
days, and after all, no dead body found.

So distinctive was Lincoln's touch that scores of stories and
observations became far better known in his version than
in the original, and some that sounded properly Lincoln-
esque were probably not his at all – for instance that saying
about fooling some of the people some of the time, and
some of them all the time, but not all of them all of the time.

It was a natural progression to good letter-writing.
Lincoln's letters were sometimes funny, sometimes warm
and sometimes devastating. Hundreds of them are reproduced in the volumes of his collected writings, including
some that, having counted to ten I suppose, he decided
not to send. I will snatch a few now. This for instance is
how he replied in 1860 to Grace Bedell, the child from
New York State who urged him to grow a beard:

My dear little Miss.

Your very agreeable letter of the 15th is received.

I regret the necessity of saying I have no daughters. I have
three sons – one seventeen, one nine, and one seven, years of
age. They, with their mother, constitute my whole family.

As to the whiskers, having never worn any, do you not
think people would call it a piece of silly affection if I were
to begin it now? Your very sincere well-wisher

A. Lincoln

Here in contrast is a smooth example, with a sting in its tail, that he wrote to General McClellan in 1862:

My dear Sir

This morning I felt constrained to order Blenker's Division to Fremont; and I write this to assure you that I did so with great pain, understanding that you would wish it otherwise. If you could know the full pressure of the case, I am confident you would justify it – even beyond a mere acknowledgement that the commander-in-chief may order what he pleases. Yours very truly

A. Lincoln

The most famous and admired of all his letters was based upon a misconception – Lincoln had been told that a Mrs Lydia Bixby of Boston had lost five sons in battle in the civil war, when in fact only two had been killed: but the letter was published in the Boston *Transcript* anyway, and proved one of Lincoln's most successful exercises in public relations, frequently quoted to this day. Here it is:

Dear Madam,-

I have been shown in the files of the War Department a statement of the Adjutant General of Massachusetts that you are the mother of five sons who have died gloriously on the field of battle. I feel how weak and fruitless must be any word of mine which should attempt to beguile you from the grief of a loss so overwhelming. But I cannot refrain from tendering you the consolation that may be found in the thanks of the Republic they died to save.

I pray that our Heavenly Father may assuage the anguish of your bereavement, and leave you only the cherished memory of the loved and lost, and the solemn pride that must be yours to have laid so costly a sacrifice upon the altar of freedom. Yours, very sincerely and respectfully

A. Lincoln

I prefer Lincoln's more down-to-earth letter-writing mode, as in this brief letter to some official or other:

Majr. Ramsay
My dear Sir
     The lady – bearer of this – says she has two sons who want to work. Set them at it, if possible. Wanting to work is so rare a merit, that it should be encouraged. Yours truly

A. Lincoln

Or this to a legal client concerned with a sale of property:

As to the real estate we cannot attend to it. We are not real estate agents, we are lawyers. We recommend that you give the charge of it to Mr Isaac S. Britton, a trustworthy man, and one whom the Lord made on purpose for such business.

But of course it was natural that the Lincoln style reached its apogee in speeches on great themes, and especially themes in which his emotions were genuinely involved. True style comes from the heart – *l'homme même*. One can devise an *ad hoc* mode of writing – brusque, witty or suitably sympathetic for a letter, clever or ironic in debate, inspiring for the hustings – but the style that expresses what the heart feels is the real thing. Oscar Wilde once flippantly remarked that in matters of grave importance style, not sincerity, was the vital factor: it was the mark of Lincoln's latent nobility as an artist, more noble at his best than Wilde could ever be, that he managed to fuse the two. One need not be spontaneous to be sincere, and nothing indeed was spontaneous about Lincoln's ultimate style. He never read Browning, and no fine careless rapture entered his oratory – his impromptu speeches were generally poor. Instead even his most pellucid sentences were assiduously honed, their words chosen with infinite labour; and that was because Lincoln knew just what his heart demanded of them.

In 1861 Seward offered him a peroration for his first inaugural address, delivered just as the civil war was about to burst upon the nation. Lincoln accepted the general gist of it, but so altered its shape and rhythm that it became unmistakeably his own. 'I close,' said Seward's first sentence. 'I am loth to close,' said Lincoln's. 'We are not,' suggested the Secretary of State, 'we must not be, aliens or enemies, but fellow-countrymen and brethren.' 'We are not enemies, but friends,' amended the President-elect. 'We must not be enemies.' The last sentence of the speech was presented by Seward thus: 'The mystic chords which, proceeding from so many battlefields and so many patriot graves, pass through all the hearts and all the hearths in this broad continent of ours, will yet harmonize in their ancient music when breathed upon by the guardian angels of the nation.' This wasn't bad. Lincoln evidently accepted its meaning, but he knew it was not quite what he felt. It was not his heart's music, and he rewrote it to become one of the best-remembered and best-loved cadences of American prose:

The mystic chords of memory, stretching from every battlefield and every patriot grave, to every living heart and hearthstone, all over this broad land, will yet swell the chorus of the Union, when again touched, as surely, they will be, by the better angels of our nature.

The cleverest of mere politicians cannot write like that: they were the better angels of Lincoln's own nature that lifted him from the oratorical commonplace into the visionary sublime – opening windows upon Russell's less fretful world, for what adjective could be less suitable than 'fretful' to describe such a passage? Many another phrase speaks to us of Lincoln's truest inner self: 'Fellow citizens, we cannot escape history' – 'We shall nobly save, or meanly lose, the last, best hope of earth' – 'If we could first know *where* we are, and *whither* we are tending, we could then judge better *what* to do, and *how* to do it' – 'With malice towards none; with charity for all; with firmness in the right, as God gives us to see the right, let us strive on to finish the work we are in; to bind up the nation's wounds; to care for him who shall have borne the battle, and for his widow, and his orphan – to do all which may achieve and cherish a just and lasting peace, among ourselves and with all nations.'

The best thing Lincoln ever did was to write the Gettysburg Address. However mean and crafty the actions he had allowed himself, in the fulfilment of his inexorable ambition, he made up for them all with 265 words of oratory in a Pennsylvania cemetery. The address certainly contained its deceptions. H. L. Mencken was famously to argue that it was not Lincoln's Northern soldiers who had sacrificed themselves in the cause of self-determination, but the Confederates; Lincoln never really subscribed to the proposition that all men were born equal; the phrase 'of the people, by the people, for the people' was almost certainly plagiarized. But the speech's inner content is all true, if only in retrospect. Lincoln's loyalty to his wretched wife, his inexhaustible love for Willie and Tad, his pride of country, his sympathy for animals, his kind understanding of ordinary people, his sadness — somehow or other, to my mind, all are miraculously instinct between the lines of this incomparable speech. He never dreamed the little piece was to live for ever — he was rather dissatisfied with it, and with its reception, too. For myself, though, when I stand outside the house on Lincoln Square, Gettysburg, where he wrote its last draft that night, I am as moved as I am by the thought of a great lyric poet, shut behind his door, working away at a sonnet.

No book about Abraham Lincoln, however slight, can decently omit the text of the Gettysburg Address, so here are all its words in the best-authenticated version:

Four score and seven years ago our fathers brought forth on this continent, a new nation, conceived in Liberty, and dedicated to the proposition that all men are created equal.

Now we are engaged in a great civil war, testing whether that nation, or any nation so conceived and so dedicated, can long endure. We are met on a great battle-field of that war. We have come to dedicate a portion of that field, as a final resting-place for those who here gave their lives that their nation might live. It is altogether fitting and proper that we should do this.

But in a larger sense, we cannot dedicate – we cannot consecrate – we cannot hallow this ground. The brave men, living or dead, who struggled here, have consecrated it, far beyond our poor power to add or detract. The world will little note, nor long remember what we say here, but it can never forget what they did here. It is for us the living, rather, to be dedicated here to the unfinished work which they who fought here have so nobly advanced. It is rather for us to be here dedicated to the great task remaining before us – that from these honored dead we take increased devotion to that cause for which they gave the last full measure of devotion – that we here highly resolve that these dead shall not have died in vain – that this nation, under God, shall have a new birth of freedom – and that government of the people, by the people, for the people, shall not perish from the earth.

The poet watching from the Washington sidewalk, as the President rode by towards the Soldiers' Home, was to be Abraham Lincoln's posthumous laureate. Perhaps Walt Whitman had Abraham in mind when he wrote about 'the large unconscious scenery of my land with its lakes and forests . . . under the arching heavens of the afternoon swift passing'; for it was part of Lincoln's artistry, if an unconscious part, that in the course of his life he became America himself. He began to look, to seem, like a personification of his country: big, grand, shambling, including in his character so much that was good and bad in it. No other country could have presented such a President to the world. I wrote myself, back on page 26, that Lincoln had always seemed like a river-man to me, but I ought to have said that he has always seemed, too, like an American river itself, sprawling across the continent with all its shallows and mudbanks, and the sweep of its open waters.

Lincoln obviously did not try to resemble America, although even in his time Uncle Sam was gradually metamorphosed into his image. He did however have a strong sense of place, and I am sure his visions of American landscape were transmuted into his views on American destiny. In his day he was thought of as a Westerner, the Middle West not yet having been identified, but in fact the greater American West was no more than an ideal to him. The nearest he ever got to the Rocky Mountains or California was Council Bluffs in Iowa, the place where, on my page 7, he is memorialized as Christ reincarnated. It was in 1859 that he went there. He owned a small tract of land in Iowa, awarded him twenty-seven years before as a veteran of the Black Hawk War. He never did anything with it, but its possession meant that it was as a patron of the soil beneath his feet, as it were, that he looked for the first time across the wide Missouri valley towards the western plains. There is a terrifically suggestive prospect still from the obelisk that marks the spot – a grand continental view, with the river running magnificently into the blue haze of the south, the vast plains limitless to the west, and at the foot of the hill, and over the Missouri, a big urban sprawl of railways and factories, Council Bluffs on the Iowa side, Omaha in Nebraska. Lincoln well realized the meaning of that spectacle, its scale and its power: four years later, as President of the United States, he named Council Bluffs as the eastern terminus of the Union Pacific Railroad, part of the system which was eventually to link the Atlantic and the Pacific shores of the Republic, by the route he had long worked for.

He carried with him through life the rough-hewn aura of the frontier – time and again we read of him picking up an axe to demonstrate his strength and his dexterity. There was a sense of great space to him, like the space of the prairies, where the Ullendorffs, the Thomases, the Wolenskis, the Smiths and the Olssens lived like islanders behind their windbreaks. Physically he was an exaggeration of all the Yankees who ever were. When the Kentucky in him showed he could have stood as a living logo of the stylish-shabby South – and even a Southerner could say of him, twenty years after his death, that he embodied in himself 'all the strength and gentleness, all the majesty and grace of the Republic'. It was apt that when he became President of a disrupted United States, and dedicated himself to putting its magnificence together again, the great dome of the Capitol was still in a tangle of scaffolding.

Most of us, if we care about the shape of our lives, hope for a graceful pattern from birth to death. Lincoln's was like an art form in itself, unfolding down the years not in sporadic jerks and bumps as most men's do, but grandly, in a steady parabola. His personal growth from backwoods boy to statesman, his political career from the provinces to the Presidency, his emotional life emerging triumphant from so many miseries and disappointments, his craftiness and deceptions resulting in a greater good, his death on a lovely spring evening at the moment of victory, four years to the day after Fort Sumter had struck its flag – all have the true Platonic harmony to them, like some of his own best prose. It was a life of hopeful fatalism, and one of his favourite passages from Pope expresses it:

> *All nature is but art, unknown to thee;*
> *All chance, direction, which thou canst not see;*
> *All discord, harmony not understood;*
> *All partial evil, universal good;*
> *And, spite of pride, in erring reason's spite,*
> *One truth is clear, whatever is, is right.*

Even his name fitted. 'Abraham' was the only name for a man who was to be rhetorically hailed as the Father of his Country, genuinely loved as the father of his troops. And it seems artistically inevitable that he should reach his Calvary on a Good Friday, when the actor John Wilkes Booth shot him in the back of the head in his box at Ford's Theater in Washington.

There had been several plots against his life, and his minders were right to be cautious. There was the conspiracy to harm him at Baltimore, on his way from Springfield at the start of his Presidency. There was a shot from an unknown marksman which went through his hat one evening when he was riding near the Soldiers'

Home. Several death threats were posted to him, and two unknown and suspicious men tried to come near him on the *Malvern*, before he sailed away from Richmond on page 175. The rules of war, which meant more than they do now, forbade any officially sponsored attempt to kill or kidnap a Head of State, but Confederates felt themselves free of this restriction anyway after an unfortunate event in 1864.

Remember that tented prison camp at Belle Isle, which Lincoln saw in the middle of the James River at Richmond? In the previous year he had been persuaded to approve a raid on the city to liberate the island's prisoners, one of its leaders being the son of his friend Admiral John Dahlgren, commander of the Union navy. The raid was a disastrous failure. Colonel Ulric Dahlgren was killed on the outskirts of Richmond, and among his papers was allegedly found a statement concerning the true purpose of the operation. It was not, it seemed, just to free the prisoners of Belle Isle: it was to assassinate Jefferson Davis, the President of the Confederacy. The Confederate Government immediately made the paper public. Northerners denounced it as a fraud, and perhaps it was; but it may have been what triggered Booth's elaborately conceived plan to murder Lincoln that night.

You can still see Ford's Theater, Lincoln's Golgotha, just as it was then. There is nothing ominous about it. It is a working theatre still, in a busy part of downtown Washington – the Hard Rock Café is just along the road. The double box where Lincoln sat with Mary and a couple of guests is still there, and you can easily imagine Booth theatrically leaping to the stage below, brandishing his pistol as an actor must, and shouting the State motto of Virginia – *Sic Semper Tyrannis* – like the last line of a thriller. The whole episode is so familiar, from picture, and history book, and novel, and movie, that it is odd to find it happening in a genuine everyday theatre, where the performance on 14 April 1865 was of *Our American Cousin*, and the performance as I write is of *Inspiration*, featuring Queen Esther Marrow and the Harlem Gospel Singers. *Our American Cousin* was a not very successful English melodrama turned into an American farce, advertised as 'an eccentric comedy' and equipped for the occasion, in the way of command performances, with some topical ad libs, on the lines of 'This reminds me of a story, as Mr Lincoln would say.' A happy President evidently enjoyed it. They say that Mary snuggled close to him during the performance, and that she wondered if it was right to make such a display of affection before their young guest Clara Harris. 'She won't think anything about it,' Lincoln replied in his last recorded words, with a squeeze of the hand, perhaps, for his poor loving wife.

The room in the house over the road, too, where they took Abraham to die, seems almost unnaturally ordinary. It is quite a small room, containing so many people in imaginative renderings of the death-scene that a book about it is subtitled *The Rubber Room Phenomenon*. The light is dim. You wonder, with a wry sadness, if the bed is really big enough to have taken Lincoln's long frame, or whether his size 14 feet hung over the end. You wonder too about William T. Clark, the lodger who usually occupied it, who was out that night and had no idea that a President was dying on his mattress. It would

take a hard heart indeed not to be moved by the thought
of Lincoln breathing his last there while the statesmen
of his Cabinet wait solemnly all around, and Mary comes
in and out all night, distraught from the room next door.

The event inspired everyone to nobility, even Lincoln's rivals. It was old Edwin Stanton's finest moment,
and among us foreigners almost all he is remembered
for, when as the martyr-President left them he murmured
to the assembled company: 'Now he belongs to the ages.'

'O Captain, my Captain!' cried Whitman. 'Sweetest,
wisest soul of all my days!' And when, a century later,
Philip Roth's Portnoy dreamed of meaningful suffering,
he thought of it as 'something perhaps along the line of
Abraham Lincoln'. If Shakespeare had written a play
about Lincoln – if only! – it would not have been one
of his history plays, but one of his dark tragedies, full of
ghosts and premonitions. It was true to this black genre that
Lincoln's final ambitions, conceived in his full maturity,
were betrayed when he died. His old opponents, the
Republican ultras, soon abandoned his plans for a mag-
nanimous re-absorption of the Confederacy into the
American Union. They wanted a South absolutely subju-
gated and governed by the North, and they set in foot
fateful policies of revenge, calling them Reconstruction.
Jefferson Davis himself they locked up for years as a traitor,
and they allowed a ragbag multitude of carpet-baggers
and profiteers, black and white, to dominate the broken
States of the South. 'With malice towards none' was forgotten, once the author of the phrase was gone. Even
Lincoln's monumental funeral, a protracted ritual which

took his corpse in a black-shrouded train from city to city back to the cemetery at Springfield – even that solemn progress, some say, was organized as an incitement to harshness against the defeated Confederates.

As for the ghosts and premonitions, Lincoln knew them well – ghosts of the dead of his victorious war, premonitions of his own end. He remained morbidly interested in death and human transience. He liked to tell the story of the eastern monarch asking his savants for a text which he could keep always in view, and which would be appropriate to every situation: '*And this, too, shall pass away*' was what the wise men gave him. Even Lincoln's own nostalgic poem about his return to the scenes of his boyhood ended dolefully:

> *I range the fields with pensive tread,*
> *And pace the hollow rooms,*
> *And feel (companion of the dead)*
> *I'm living in the tombs.*

Probably the only opera Lincoln ever saw, in New York in 1863, was Verdi's *Un Ballo Maschero* – all about an assassination. More than once he referred prophetically to his own murder, and in 1864 he had a vatic dream which has to it all the hallmarks of an exhausted imagination, belaboured for three fearful years by images of death. 'There seemed to be a death-like stillness about me.' Ward Lamon remembered him telling it:

Then I heard subdued sobs, as if a number of people were weeping. I thought I left my bed and wandered downstairs

. . . I kept on until I entered the East Room, which I entered. There I met a sickening surprise. Before me was a catafalgue, on which was a corpse wrapped in funeral vestments . . . Who is dead in the White House? I demanded of one of the soldiers. 'The President,' was the answer. 'He was killed by an assassin!' Then came a loud burst of grief from the crowd, which awoke me from my dream . . . I slept no more than night.

But I believe earlier intimations of mortality – and immortality – came at the Great Western depôt at Springfield, that damp morning in 1861 when Abraham, having written his labels with his own hand, stepped upon the train of his destiny. The station still stands, near the Sheriff's office, and often enough a freight train comes lumbering by, wailing its whistle constantly as it passes through the city streets. The speech Lincoln made then, having inevitably passed into the folk-repertoire of Springfield, is inscribed in full upon a metal plaque.

I find it the most touching of all his works, because it is so redolent of all goodbyes, and because we know now that Lincoln would never come back to Springfield. It brought tears to my eyes when I read it there one morning – in a drizzle too, as it happened, beside the Monroe Street level crossing, over the road from the Sheriff's parked police cars. I wish I could say that as I read it one of those trains came howling through: but no, when I had finished and looked north and south along the track, there was nothing to be seen, only a few wagons in a siding, and the long straight empty rails – Ford's Theater one way, Sinking Spring the other.

Conclusions: You May Be Right

Grape jelly, which I so distrusted at the start of this book, has its American critics nowadays. 'The tragic result of being forced to confront grape jelly morning after morning,' wrote the American humorist Gerard Nachman in 1997, 'is that, eventually, you just give up and, what's really depressing, start eating it without even thinking.' I gather the sixteenth President is not quite the saint he was, either. I recently asked a young man at Baby Bull's Café, at New Salem, what he thought of Abraham Lincoln. 'I'll tell you,' he said, 'there's an older guy I met, he was telling me he remembered some gentlemen who remembered people who knew Lincoln – you know what I'm saying? – and they said *he wasn't a very good individual*. Know what I mean?' 'I see where you're coming from,' said I, falling once more into the vernacular.

America does not change as fast as Europe, but it is much altered all the same since I first went there in the

1950s, and its enthusiasms are now far more readily directed at rock stars, actors and baseball players than at dead statesmen. When in 1998 I asked a woman at Springfield if just now and then she didn't tire of the Lincoln memory she replied with a sigh that I didn't know the half of it. By then not all the inquiries on Abraham Lincoln websites were flattering to the Great Emancipator. 'Abe was not a good man,' one fifteen-year-old went on-line to tell the nation. 'Your little hero boy was the cause of the seperation of the North and South. Why don't you find some real person for a hero like Martin Luther King Jr or Princess Diana.' Among upholders of States Rights, who include some violent fanatics, Lincoln is seen to this day as a betrayer of the Founding Fathers. Blacks often blame him for the fact that racial prejudice and discrimination is still rife in the United States, not least in the North, and they do not remember kindly his views on white supremacy – 'those old guys said,' concluded my informant at Baby Bull's, 'that he weren't not much more than a white cracker racist.' In America, at the start of the twenty-first century, to speak admiringly of the Lincoln record is not invariably considered politically correct.

Abroad, where I come from, the legend remains more or less intact. It was never quite so hysterical anyway, of course, and is more or less frozen in the paradigm of the Gettysburg Address. Few foreigners think badly of Abraham Lincoln. Across the world his statues still stand in square and public garden. In Tokyo there is a Lincoln Centre. In Denmark there is a Lincoln Memorial Log Cabin. This morning I asked three Welsh people what

were their impressions of Abraham Lincoln, and all three
used the word 'good' in their replies – like Karl Marx,
they had absorbed him into their consciousness as an
example of an almost extinct breed, the great man who
was also good. I suppose it is true to say that he is still
better remembered in the world at large, his image more
vivid and his reputation more generally revered, than
any other politician of history.

Asked about his historical effect, foreigners are likely
to be more hesitant. Africans and Asians may speak vaguely
of him as a liberator, an archetypal anti-colonialist. Some
Europeans will respectfully remember him as the man
who, by saving the Union, established American democracy as the lodestar of all political aspiration. If it were
not for Lincoln's victory in the civil war, others will
maintain, there might not have been a USA capable of
pulling so many European irons out of the fire. But for
myself I think of his legacy to the world as equivocal:
and perhaps Puccini did, too, when in 1904 he made the
cad Benjamin Franklin Pinkerton, USN, sail to the ruin
of Madame Butterfly in a battleship named *Abraham
Lincoln*.

For one thing, it seems to me from far away, Lincoln led
his country into the miserable arena of international
rivalry from which the idealistic Founding Fathers had
tried to extract it. As I understand it Jefferson, their
genius, had imagined an America peaceful, modest, rural,
devolved, its authority equably distributed among its
separate States, its defence provided by the patriotism
of the people themselves, with their muskets over the

fireplace in the kitchen – a federation of friends and colleagues classical in aesthetic, tolerant in morality, far removed from the cauldron of war and internecine feuding which had bedevilled Europe for so many centuries. Power and Liberty, Jefferson thought, did not go together.

Lincoln found them uneasy comrades too, but it was he nevertheless who made a centralized Power of the Republic. His only war aim, he said at first, was to keep the Union intact – but what kind of an aim was that? Merely the maintenance, by force, of one big Power rather than two smaller ones. He made it seem a mystic compulsion: 'The Union! The Union!' he repeatedly breathes, almost ectoplasmically, in D. W. Griffith's film of his life. But it was really what we now call nationalism, edging into imperialism: not patriotism, which merely means love of country, but a more grandiose notion of national identity. He foresaw 'a vast future' for his Republic. It was under his leadership that the United States became a singular compound noun – the US is, rather than the US are – and Americans acquired a taste for militarism. 'We are getting the hang of the game,' said one of John Hay's friends during the civil war, 'and rather like it.' America would be 'a nation of soldiers', prophesied Seward the Secretary of State, and one day the whole of the American continent would fall 'within the magic circle of the American Union'. Said General Hooker of the American future: 'We shall be the greatest military power on earth, greatest in numbers, in capability, in dash, in spirit, in intelligence of the soldiery.' Already, by the end of the civil war, Lincoln was Commander-in-Chief of the biggest army in existence and a navy of 671 warships, supported by a huge expanding industrial base – a consummation that would have satisfied a Napoleon or a Bismarck, and challenged the purplest hyperboles of British imperialism. When Richmond fell in 1865, 900 guns fired a victory salute in Washington.

America could already be seen as a potential arbiter of the world, and I suspect Lincoln wanted it so. He was convinced that the American way of government was superior to all others. It was the last best hope of earth. He had been brought up to think this, brainwashed by the visionary ethos of the 1775 Revolution against the British, and seemed oblivious to the possibility that other peoples might prefer other systems. The one blot on the American escutcheon had been the existence of slavery, and now that the slaves were emancipated Americans could survey the whole planet assured that their methods of life and governance were the best, and must be the envy of everyone.

As individuals modern Americans seem to me almost miraculously free of arrogance and chauvinism, but as a nation they have never lost that sense of superiority, and the instinct for interference that goes with it. Nor have they lost their fascination with warlike things, their love of weapons and their respect for military leaders. By the last decades of the twentieth century it might well be said that theirs was one of the most militarist States on earth, and perhaps the most innately imperialist. Unchallengeable as it had then become as the one Super-Power, contemptuous of the United Nations, it seemed more convinced than ever that its way was the only right way, to be distributed willy-nilly among the lesser States. This was, of course, an old delusion of power. In their time half the nations of Europe, not to mention all the Ozymandic empires of Asia, had believed themselves the only author-ized messengers of truth, and God-ordained to police it. Now the End of History must be American-style capitalist democracy – a form of democracy, incidentally, in which the President of the Republic was far closer in power and status to King George III in 1775 than to contemporary European heads of State. 'What was *this*?' an American Ranger remembered asking himself incredulously, when Somali gunmen had the temerity to fire upon his heli-copter over Mogadishu in 1993. 'We were *Americans*!'

One could argue that this was just how the Union forces thought of themselves, when they stormed through the South of the 1860s. 'They don't understand us,' as those citizens of Charleston were still telling me a century later. The modern American sense of privilege, so irritat-ing to foreigners today, and the belief that the USA has the right – the duty indeed – to intervene in the affairs of other cultures, had its origins in Lincoln's victory. When squabbling leaders from afar are summoned to Washington to settle their differences, when American statesmen fly in among their grim-faced bodyguards to warring provinces on the other side of the world, I think of him stalking with his marines through the ruins of Richmond.

But in Richmond he had Tad by the hand, and he was sick of war. By 1865 his aims were purified. He wanted an end to slavery, he wanted a return to peace and friendship among his people – that was all. He had promised Mary that when the war was over they would go a-travelling, to see the great world and all its marvels for themselves: not I am sure in any spirit of display or patronage, but simply for the pleasure of it – just as most American travellers today seldom think of themselves as citizens of the only Super-Power, and in fact are far more unassertive tourists than they were a generation ago. I may be unfair, for making Lincoln the originator of American hubris: but bewitched though I have been by his personality, in the course of thinking and writing about him, and truly loving though I have become in many ways, I am still not quite sure in my responses. I still don't know whether he deserves to be sanctified, or whether I was right to couple him, all those years ago, with a specious kind of jam. A life that I have seen as an unconscious work of art could also be interpreted as a mere series of equations, or a deliberate repertoire. Was he truly fulfilled only in his noblest prose? Confucius said of himself that he had never achieved full sincerity, and perhaps Lincoln reached it only in his brief moments of creative inspiration. Perhaps absolute sincerity is what true greatness is, and why it takes us as close as we can ever be to whatever we think of as God.

In the same year, 1953, that I first encountered Lincoln on his home ground I came across an American quotation that I have cherished ever since. It seems that Ed Murrow the broadcaster, pestered by fractious critics with complaints or finicky corrections, had devised a *pro forma* reply. I have often used it myself, and when readers of this book remonstrate with me about misjudgements, or misinterpretations, or misunderstandings of the American way, or if that lady in the California café on page 8 chances to come across these conclusions, I shall fall back once again upon its formula. Dear Sir or Madam, I shall say as Murrow did, you may be right.

A Chronological Index of the Events of Abraham Lincoln's Life Mentioned in this Book

Thomas 'Tad' Lincoln died of tuberculosis in 1871. Mary Todd Lincoln died in 1882. Robert Lincoln died in 1926, leaving no male heir. His two daughters produced, between them, two sons and a daughter, but none of these great-grandchildren of the President had children of their own. The direct Lincoln line thus came to an end with the death of Robert Todd Lincoln Beckwith on Christmas Eve, 1985.

Index